TRANSITIONS

TRANSITIONS

Selected Writings by The Creative
Writing Group of American Association
of University Women, Arizona's
Northwest Valley Branch

GRETA MANVILLE, EDITOR

iUniverse, Inc.
Bloomington

TRANSITIONS
SELECTED WRITINGS BY THE CREATIVE WRITING GROUP OF AMERICAN ASSOCIATION OF UNIVERSITY WOMEN, ARIZONA'S NORTHWEST VALLEY BRANCH

iUniverse books may be ordered through booksellers or by contacting:

iUniverse
1663 Liberty Drive
Bloomington, IN 47403
www.iuniverse.com
1-800-Authors (1-800-288-4677)

ISBN: 978-1-4620-2616-6 (sc)
ISBN: 978-1-4620-2617-3 (ebk)

Printed in the United States of America

iUniverse rev. date: 06/20/2011

Contents

Introduction

Vivian Wood

Our Creative Writing Group, an American Association of University Women's special interest group, has been in existence around a quarter of a century—perhaps longer. In 1992, the group published *Reflection on Retirement Living*, a collection of members' writings. At that time, the writers were known simply as the Writers' Group.

Over the years, membership has fluctuated and we acquired a new name. Always the members have in common their love of writing, as reflected in our stated purpose:

To awaken or reawaken our creativity as writers
To share our writing efforts and interests
To receive critical evaluations and to critique the works of others
To grow in our knowledge of the craft of writing
To learn of current contests and market opportunities
To share publication experiences

ADVENTURES

The Aleutian Islands

Judy Neigoff

Why would anyone want to go to the Aleutian Islands? No towns, no trees, miserable weather. Even "no shopping," as one of my friends pointed out in horror. No, there really isn't much to recommend this lonely chain of islands that sweeps across the Pacific Ocean from Alaska to Russia. Maybe a million years ago when they formed a land bridge that the ancestral Native Americans crossed, but not today. Today they are treeless islands with no inhabitants, constant high winds and rain, and summer temperatures in the 40's.

But here I was—about to embark on a two-week vacation cruise of the Aleutian Islands. It was the summer of 1996, and my Mother and I were on the World Discoverer, an icebreaker cruise ship that we had previously taken to Greenland and Iceland, and another time to Antarctica. This year the ship was going to the Aleutian Islands so my Mother decreed that this is where we were going to go.

There were eighty-six other foolish passengers on the cruise with us. The group was roughly divided into three groups. First, there were some people like us who wanted just to get away from civilization and had already traveled to the more logical places on earth. Then we discovered the crazy birders. It seems there is a contest for birders in which they attempt to spot every bird in the world. The first person who does this wins. These serious birders were here to add the species of birds that only live in the Aleutian Islands to their list. Finally, we met the group of WWII vets who were here to revisit their old abandoned bases on Attu and Kiska. I hadn't known there were WWII battles fought on American soil here.

And so we set off on our journey. We started at the far end of the chain just off the coast of Russia. Attu was the first stop, where we toured the eerily empty American military base. It had been abandoned only recently when the end of the Cold War and the use of remote satellite surveillance technology made it unnecessary to have a base so near to Russia. We saw roads with no cars, housing units with no open doors, recreation centers, mess halls, chapel and hospital, all empty but in perfect condition. There was a "For Sale" sign on the base! The American government was willing to sell the base—cheap—to be used as a town for civilians, but, alas, there were no takers. That night's dinner conversation on the ship was, "What group of American citizens we would like to see settled in Attu." I thought it would do well as a prison. Crime would certainly go down if offenders knew they would be sent here.

The next day we landed on Kiska. What a difference. Here all we saw was the derelict remains of the WWII base. There was an old wooden dock with holes in it and fallen-down Quonset huts. The ship's tour leader asked us to refrain from wandering too far afield because there could still be unexploded land mines about. That kept us together! I particularly liked the burned out shell of a Japanese submarine we found at the water's edge. But the emotional highlight of this island was the Kiska National Forest. The soldiers stationed here during WWII planted a few fir trees in a sheltered cove and worked hard to nurture and protect them. For a touch of humor they put up a sign that said "Kiska National Forest." Some of these same soldiers, now on this trip fifty years later, were overjoyed to see that the trees were still here and had grown to a whopping six feet high. After dinner the vets gave us a fascinating blow-by-blow tale of the long ago battle here.

The following days were for the birders. We landed at several islands where the birders with their binoculars and notebooks headed out through the tall grasses looking for their species. The rest of us just took in the scene and tried to stay warm, dry, and out of the wind. You could say it was a beautiful landscape if you like stark emptiness. The grasses were very tall and green and were usually bent over in the wind. No trees (except the Kiska National Forest) could grow on these cold, rocky, windy islands. Also there were no animals. It was strange not to see even a squirrel or chipmunk. But there were plenty of birds. With no natural enemies they thrive here. When the birders returned we got an earful about the red-tipped Aleutian Bunting or the green-throated whatevers that they saw. Our evening's lectures these nights were like long-winded fish stories, detailing the birders' methods of tracking and bemoaning the birds that got away.

While the birders were birding and the vets were reminiscing, the rest of the passengers could watch the kitchen crew go fishing. Huge flounders were being caught and cooked for dinner. Mom loved the fresh fish. Also the captain was giving navigation lessons on the bridge. I was often up there trying to understand the squiggly lines on the ocean charts. Every day those who wanted to brave the weather could set out in a Zodiac and watch whales and sea birds. It was fun as long as we knew that a hot shower and dry clothing awaited us back on the ship.

When we finally reached the islands closer to the shore of Alaska, the islands held more life. Remains of Native American villages could be seen. Evidence of small rodents could be found. Bushes existed among the grasses. We were getting back to real nature here. We passengers were slowly primed to re-enter the real world again.

If you ever get a chance to travel to the Aleutian Islands, don't. Unless, of course, you are a birder, a WWII Aleutian vet, or crazy travelers like my mother and me.

A Senior Woman Travels Alone to New York City

Ann Winsor

Why would a single woman, 85 years old and in her right mind, even consider going to the huge metropolitan city of New York, particularly since she did not know a soul there? First, there's the spirit of adventure, aided by a free round-trip ticket. Add to that the need to get out of a community of my older neighbors, who are very nice, but it is refreshing to mingle with younger persons—to come in contact with new ideas and to be challenged with current concerns.

How did I get the free round-trip ticket? It all began with the purchase of my new hearing aid, which cost me the tidy sum of $3,400. Not being one to wander around with that kind of money in my wallet, I put the amount on my MasterCard, which added to my Delta SkyMiles and won for me the much-desired free round-trip plane ticket.

Since it was important for me to reserve a room in a CHEAP hotel, I got on the internet, connected with CheapTickets.com which found me a room with shared bathroom at a hotel for $115 a day. It was conveniently located in midtown, where I could be within walking distance to most places. This way, I could avoid expensive cab fares costing $2.50 the minute one enters the cab. I would be wearing my gym sneakers that showed a lot of wear since I regularly put in two miles a day at a 15-minute rate to a mile on the treadmill. I certainly was in good shape to walk a New York City mile.

About the luggage—all I had was a roomy purse and a backpack in which I squeezed one set of underwear, two scarves, a flannel nightie (it does get chilly at night even in the summer), a pair of flat-heeled shoes for going out to special places, and a collapsible umbrella. Wearing a black trench coat and a felt cowboy hat and gloves, I was ready. My wallet held 200 dollars and, of course, the important MasterCard. I also included a copy of *Steinbeck: A Life in Letters*. John Steinbeck would be my companion for the times when I could sit or lie down in my hotel room. Connecting with such a talented writer made me feel less alone—and I would be in the city where he made his final home.

After I arrived in New York and exited the plane, I boarded a bus that took me from the Newark Airport to a bus stop near Grand Central Station. With the address of the hotel in my hands, I was advised that 51st Street and Second Avenue is within walking distance, so I headed out. Fortunately, there was only a light, gentle drizzle, not at all a problem, since I had little to carry. It was a nice, brisk walk to the hotel. As I hurried along, I kept checking with passersby to confirm that I was going in the right direction. Everyone was courteous and after about 15 minutes, there it was! A modest hotel, right around the corner from the 17th precinct of the New York Police Department with many police cars parked nearby. The neighborhood looked friendly. Outside the restaurants, tables were set up, with folks laughing, eating, and drinking under the sheltered canopies and awnings. So this would be my home for a week, good!

The lobby was deserted except for one woman who was chatting with the desk clerk. I approached, gave my name and told him I had reserved a room for a week. He stated the price—$115 a night.

"But I am a senior citizen," I said, "85 years old. Certainly, I deserve a discount and, what's more, if you can read what's in front of you, it's because someone like me, a first-grade teacher, taught you how."

He listened and after some thought, with much rolling of his eyes, lowered the price to $99.

Noticing a certain accent in his speech, I asked, "Where are you from? What country?"

"Colombia," he replied. "Do you know where it is?"

I responded, "No, I don't know where it is."

He flashed back at me, "Oops, the price of the room goes up to $115."

Using all the charm I could muster, I pleaded, "Oh, please don't do that. $99 is as much as I can afford. Let's keep it at $99."

He finally capitulated and agreed to lower the price.

*　　*　　*

I was off to the waiting elevator, no bellhop necessary since my bags were either in my hand or on my back. As the elevator creaked along, I looked around at my shabby surroundings. This certainly was not a classy place, but good enough for the short time I would be here.

After much grinding and squeaking, the old elevator stopped and off I went, checking the numbers on the rooms, noticing the threadbare carpeting and dingy walls. Finally arriving at my room, my key fit the lock, and there I was in a tiny closet of a room just wide enough to allow for the width of one window. I did have a bathroom—shared with the adjacent roomer. Three days went by, however, before the maid told me about this bathroom. I had been schlepping down the hall to a community toilet and shower.

As I looked out the window, thousands of lights from the tall skyscrapers glittered. The view convinced me that, yes, I was indeed in the city of New York. Alone—and filled with a sense of adventure about exploring my new surroundings. Who knows what interesting persons I might meet, and what experiences lay ahead?

But first I must eat, having gone without a meal since leaving Phoenix. This would give me a chance to explore the neighborhood. After inquiring from the hotel concierge about nearby eateries, I wandered outside to check his advice. Next to the hotel was an Italian place that looked inviting.

I seated myself, looked around and could see that everyone was paired off in couples. Whenever I am in a situation like this, pangs of being alone really make me uncomfortable. It seems the whole world is made up of couples—everywhere!

After reading the menu, the most reasonable meal was spaghetti and meatballs, standard fare for an Italian restaurant. I ordered a glass of merlot. It was the bitterest wine I have ever tasted. I slowly sipped it while waiting for the spaghetti, which turned out to be as bad as the wine, and tasteless. I left, leaving much of the meal behind, and headed back to my room.

Curling up on the bed with my Steinbeck book, the window still ablaze with lights, I read myself to sleep.

Cozy and rested by the following day, I ventured down to Times Square. I bought a ticket for the New York City Official Heritage Tour, a double-decker bus that allowed me to view the tall skyscrapers and to sit close to the guide while she described each important site as she drove. We were allowed to get off at whatever stop we wished, to be picked up later at the same place.

My first stop was the South Street Seaport Museum. I assumed I would be allowed to view various vessels but instead heard a lecture on the poet, Walt Whitman, who wrote *Leaves of Grass*. This very talented poet lived in nearby Brooklyn. No one would publish his first book of poems. Finally, a friend relented and said, "If you can learn how to operate my printing press, we will print it." And that is what Whitman did.

Later, I wandered about the piers and climbed back on the next bus, stopping at Chinatown. What a busy crowded place! All sorts of shops and restaurants, babies in carriages, and everyone talking very loud. I felt as though I had been transported to China. Everything was priced cheaply, so I finally bought a wristwatch for $10, one that had no figures, just twelve, straight up.

Next to Chinatown was Little Italy, so I stopped and had a fine lunch with some good wine. Not really knowing what to order, I had simply beckoned to the waiter and pointed to the meal the neighbor at the next table appeared to enjoy, and I ordered that.

Beginning to tire, I got back on the bus and stopped on Madison Avenue to buy a bottle of wine. All the wines were so expensive that I finally asked the manager if he had any reasonably priced wines in stock.

He smiled and said, "These wines are not expensive, I have some bottles that cost $1,000 and up."

I gasped and quietly commented, "What expensive urine that would make."

Finally deciding on a bottle of merlot, I hiked back to my room and having also bought a sandwich at one of the many delicatessens, I sipped my wine and enjoyed my sandwich, while gazing out the window at the exciting lights.

*   *   *

The next day, I wandered down 42nd Street, ten blocks from my hotel, joined a line of ticket purchasers and chose to see, *I Love You, You're Perfect, Now Change*. These tickets were available at attractive prices since they had not been sold by the previous night. No checks were accepted, nor credit cards, which meant I had to pull up my sweater to retrieve the cash in my money belt, personal modesty not withstanding.

Now armed with my ticket, my next challenge was to actually locate this Off Broadway theater. Since I have no feelings of reserve, asking policemen for directions was fun. They are so young, so handsome, and ever so polite. When I was advised to take a cab, I was quick to say that I preferred walking. They appeared rather skeptical, walking—at my age? No need to tell them that I also downhill ski. I adore being challenged. I am fully convinced that is what keeps us forever young and eager to learn new ideas.

Finding the theater proved quite a hike but this gave me time to look around and view more of the city.

Arriving at the theater earlier than the performance enabled me to politely request a front seat since I have hearing issues. The play was excellent but best of all was the violinist who showed off her talents. She was also comical and kept us in stitches. Usually musicians take a minor role in plays. My daughter, who is also a musician, tells me that these musicians are paid very well and these gigs are hard to come by.

Afterward, I went into Saks and bought a suit jacket. By opening an account, I received ten percent off. I treated myself to Chanel No. 5. You only live once, and I am worth it!

*　　*　　*

The final day, I spent a memorable few hours at Grand Central Station, where Scottish bagpipers performed a concert to honor the New York City Policemen. I was deeply moved by the sincere appreciation NewYorkers have for these brave men who protect them from criminals, manage to control traffic, and have a host of other duties.

At The Guggenheim Museum, I enjoyed my final day, feasting my eyes on the art collected by Catherine the Great of Russia, nine centuries of priceless beauty.

*　　*　　*

Looking back on my week and pondering the comparison of living in Sun City West, a retirement community in the desert, with the high voltage excitement of New York City, I gained perspective on my life. I value the social support of the church I attend, the coziness of my neighbors, and the safety I sense while surrounded by others near my age, with similar problems connected with aging. The return to Arizona was like coming to a real home—where I am known, respected, protected. The trip would have been ever so much better if I'd had a companion, a friend with whom to share thoughts and experiences, with whom I could laugh. Maybe next time?

Hiking the Havasaupi Canyon to Havasu Falls

Bonnie Boyce-Wilson

Sandy and I knew each other casually as we attend the same church in our Arizona retirement community. She approached me one Sunday to say she heard that I had hiked the Inca Trail to Machu Picchu. When I acknowledged that I had, she told me that she had always wanted to hike the Grand Canyon and wondered if I would consider a hike there together. She said she was not an experienced hiker, but considered herself physically fit and was determined to make this hike if she could find a companion. Sandy was counting on my experience to help her make this trek.

Sandy decided to take a few shorter hikes as a guest with my hiking group to gain experience. She bought hiking boots and socks, a hiking stick, and other gear. Meanwhile, we explored the logistics, weather, and our schedules before deciding that we would hike the Havasu Canyon in April.

Havasu Canyon is a southwestern branch of the Grand Canyon. The AAA guide book cautions: the "very rugged terrain is accessible only on horseback, by helicopter, or on foot down a precipitous trail only recommended for experienced hikers in good physical condition. The return climb out of the canyon is very arduous." The trail is nine miles down to the lodge, then another three miles beyond to see the falls. We would rent a room in the lodge at the Native American village called Supai. Young people hiking there often camp out, but for us the comfort of a motel room was the only way to go.

Day 1

As I pulled into Sandy's driveway, she was waiting at her door. We loaded up and drove north along I-17. The traffic was relatively light and we made good time, chatting comfortably about family and church. The terrain changed as we headed north, gaining elevation out of the desert with its saguaro cactus and heading into the red rock area near Sedona. Taking the old Route 66 exit, we arrived in Seligman. We immediately saw the motel sign, and were surprised at how nice it looked, freshly painted and with new doors on the rooms. The internet gave it two stars, but it was clean and comfortable.

The inexperienced motel clerk tried his best to check us in promptly. He said there were two restaurants in town, the Road Kill and Westward Lilo's. Our room was chilly as the heat was off. We turned up the thermostat and then took turns revolving like a rotisserie in front of the wall heater to get warm.

Sandy suggested we walk to the Road Kill restaurant a few blocks away. There was an extensive menu, with items labeled like animals killed on the road. Their motto is "Fresh and Tender, Right Off of Your Fender." Meals had titles like "Elk Melt" and "Muck of Duck," a bit off-putting, but the food was good. They did not serve elk or duck, as the terms implied but actually beef and chicken dishes. We finished our meals with pie, which was delicious, especially served warm with ice cream! Our waitress was friendly, had lived there most of her life, and answered our questions about the road to the trailhead.

Day 2

The alarm sounded and Sandy jumped into the shower. I dressed and began to load things in the car, packing my backpack for the hike. There was frost on the car as the temperature was 24 degrees. Despite the cold, the car started easily and we drove to Westward Lilo's café. It had a welcome sign in German and was decorated in a funky mix of Western with a German flair. There were lace curtains on the windows and various kitchen items arranged in groupings on the wall, along with rifles, deer horns and western pictures.

Leaving Seligman, we drove west on historic Route 66. There were even old "Burma Shave" signs. We turned right on Forest Service Road 18, onto the Indian Reservation. As we started down the road, the sign said 60 miles to the trailhead. I checked the remaining fuel and decided we were cutting it too close. Round trip would be one 120 miles and there were no gas stations on this road. I should have filled up in Seligman and was kicking myself for such a foolish mistake. It was 30 miles back to Seligman. We filled up the car and I bought a cup of hot tea for the road. I was no longer carrying my purse, as it was locked in the trunk, but I had my wallet in the backpack so got it out to pay. We started back, but we were now an hour later than we planned. The road was paved and fairly well maintained. The area was marked as open range and we saw cattle grazing on the sparse high desert grass.

We arrived at the Hualapai Hilltop, found the trailhead and followed the sign to visitors' parking. The place was a beehive of activity. More than fifty horses and mules were tied up, waiting to be loaded with supplies to transport down the trail. We eagerly jumped out of the car to take photos. The vista was breathtaking. We were standing on the relatively even terrain at the edge of the canyon. The sheer rock wall fell away abruptly below us, down to the floor of the canyon. The variations in colors were spectacular: bright reds, oranges and purples, in lights and shadows, with the sky above so very blue with no obstruction by haze or pollution. We could see in the far distance the tiny ribbon of trail along the bottom of the canyon. We felt awed and insignificant with such splendor all around.

The tribal people here are called Havasu Baaja, "The People of the Blue-Green Water." We stepped inside a small trailer, used as the parking lot office, where a Native American man told us we could go on down the trail and buy our Tribal Permit at the lodge. He also pointed out the toilets, which were rustic. The fixtures looked like regular ceramic toilets but were a chemical toilet, I supposed, as there was no running water. There were no doors and no roof. The tin walls were about shoulder high.

Back at the car, we pulled out our packs and water bottles, testing the outdoor temperature to decide how much clothing we needed to wear. Even though it was now 11 a.m., it still felt cool so we put on layers. We double-checked the trunk to be sure we had everything, closed the lid, and headed out. As we walked across the parking lot to the trailhead, we watched the bustle of loading supplies from two large semi-trailer size containers where supplies are stored as they are delivered. The packers took the boxes and crates out of the trailers, loading them on the packsaddles, trying to balance the weight evenly on each side of the animal. All the supplies needed by the village below are carried in by these pack trains or flown in by helicopter. The helicopter landing pad is another cleared area near the parking lots. An animal's load might look like two large boxes stacked on either side and a fifth box on top of the saddle, all five tied together snugly. Some of the "boxes" are cases of water or soda; others are canned goods, paper products or crates of mail. As the animals are loaded, they are tied to each other with lead ropes. There are about ten animals in each group. The driver rides a horse to lead the group.

Sandy and I paused often to take pictures of the panorama before us as we set off down the trail. The canyon and valley below looked very deep and the views were spectacular. God's creation is beautiful! The trail here is a long series of switchbacks down the side of the canyon wall. It is steep and the trail is covered with gravel and small loose stones. We took our time, watching for safe footing for each step, using our hiking poles for balance. We stepped aside often for the pack trains going up and down the trail. We could usually hear them coming in time for us to find a safe waiting area off the trail. We paused from time to time to look back up to the starting point, trying to locate the trail head, taking photos. It was amazing how quickly we were descending. At our stops, we drank water, finding that it was easier to hand each other the water from the other's pack, rather than trying to pull the bottles from our own packs.

As we came down from the steepest part of the canyon, just past noon, we found a small picnic area and decided it was a good place for lunch. The picnic area was a smoothed out place at the side of the trail, with some stones built up like a fence and a stone seating area. Other hikers passed us, waved or gave a friendly greeting. We were first passed by a group of four men from Atlanta, who said they had just hiked the trails at the visitor center at the Grand Canyon National Park and now had come to give this one a try. These fellows were younger than we, perhaps in their early thirties, robust looking and tan as though they enjoy an active life style. A few minutes later, two young men came up the trail, one from New Mexico and the other from New Zealand. We called out a greeting to them and asked about their hike. They took a picture for us and we reciprocated.

Next, a Native American woman and a young boy came by. I offered him a cookie from my lunch, which he eagerly accepted.

His mother, like moms everywhere, said to him, "Now, what do you say?"

He grinned. "Thanks."

Resuming our trek, we found that after the first two miles of steeper terrain which we had just completed, the trail was descending more gradually, but rocks and gravel still slowed our progress. We hiked across the valley floor, finding that the canyon narrowed abruptly and began a sharper descent. The walls here were not high, just a few feet, but as we progressed, they rapidly became much higher and soon towered above us as we moved deeper into the canyon. More pack trains and hikers came by in both directions. One group of young people on their way up chatted briefly with us and we asked about the falls. They described the beauty, the vivid colors, the bright turquoise color of the water and the neon green of the spring buds on the trees.

Sandy was too warm. Though she had earlier reversed her vest so that the fleece side was away from her body, the vest was causing her to overheat. Her T-shirt was soaked! She took off her pack and the vest, now down to her T-shirt. I hung her vest from the outside strap of my pack. She put her pack back on and was much more comfortable. We admired the scenery and began to wonder how far we had come, hoping that we might see the village as we rounded each corner of the canyon, but it was yet to be. Finally I asked one of the pack train drivers and he said it was about three more miles! The terrain was rockier now as we were following a dry streambed and must more carefully pick our way. We were surprised to notice a small patch of snow along the north-facing wall of the canyon. It was still cold here! We were keenly aware of the hazards of a flash flood. If a heavy downpour sent water rushing down this deep narrow canyon, we would have little time to scramble to higher ground. Though grateful for the cloudless sky overhead, we kept our ears open for the sound of rushing water.

I joked with Sandy, "Are we there yet?"

It was about three p.m. and we began to worry about arriving before dark. The hour delay in our start was beginning to catch up with us. We found ever-increasing rockiness in the streambed, with larger rocks to climb over or around. As another pack train came by, I asked what time it gets dark.

The driver smiled and said, "Oh, about 6:30. Don't worry, you'll make it."

The valley zigzags at every corner. Finally we saw a sign that said two miles to the village. Good news or bad? We had hoped we were closer than that. We kept putting one foot in front of the other, encouraging each other. As the canyon veered to the left, the floor of the canyon widened a bit and the trail became sandier and less rocky. The going was a bit easier because we were not in fear of being tripped by the rocks, but walking in the sand presented its own challenges, each step pulling on our boots. We could now faintly hear the water from Havasu Creek. A sign told us to take the bridge over the creek and on to the village. Later, we saw another sign pointing in the opposite direction that said the trailhead is six miles. We hoped this didn't mean that we had two more miles to go from this point. We thought the two-mile marker was a while back! The stream was running beside us, but we were so weary we hardly noticed it. My pack started to pull to the right and Sandy tried to help me reposition it. Would we ever get there?

Finally, through the trees we saw the first house at the edge of the village. It was a welcome sight, but we still must walk the entire length of the village, at least another mile, before reaching the lodge. The village was a series of houses and outbuildings; each house had an acre or so of land. Corrals held horses, mules, cows, and lots of dogs. There was a school with a large chain link fence. Near the school, kids kicked a soccer ball around the field. There were kids all around, many riding bikes. About four hundred and fifty people lived here. There were two grocery stores, a museum, a computer lab, and two churches. As we reached the town center, a hiker told us how to get to the lodge, but we still missed the turn.

A young girl on her bicycle came from the rear and asked where we are going.

"The lodge," we said.

She pointed. "It is behind you." Then she offered, "Just keep going and turn straight."

We smiled at her directions, but headed back and saw where we needed to turn. We arrived at the lodge, only to discover the lodge office closed! It closed at five and it was now a quarter past. We knocked on the manager's door and she gave us a key, telling us we could check in tomorrow.

Looking at the two-story lodge, Sandy said, wearily, "I hope we don't have an upstairs room!"

We let ourselves into the room and dropped our packs, taking off our heavy hiking boots and praying our thanks. But there was no time to rest. The café takes the last food orders at 5:45, and we did not want to miss out. I looked for my wallet to pay for dinner and could not find it. As we were pressed for time, Sandy offered to buy my dinner. More comfortable now in our tennis shoes, we walked over to the café, entered and studied the menu on the board above the cash register. The menu was not extensive, but they had a veggie burger, which pleased Sandy. I ordered a bean burrito with a small salad. We were surprised that the meals were not more expensive, given the effort to haul the supplies down the canyon. Other hikers were eating there, as well as some locals. We chatted with the men from Atlanta, comparing our experiences from the downhill trail today. Of course, they made it down much faster than we did!

We walked back to the room and adjusted the drapes for more privacy. Some of the drapery hooks were missing so they sagged a bit, and we were only partially successful. The room was comfortable and spacious, with basic furnishings. There was no TV or phone. Sandy showered and got in bed. I finished my journal for the day and jumped into the shower. Boy! Did that warm water feel good!

I searched more carefully and was now convinced that I did not have my wallet. It had my driver's license, a credit card, and cash. The last time I remembered using it was at the gas station. I believed I took the wallet back to the car when I bought the cup of tea, and usually would have put it in my purse, but since I was no longer carrying my purse, the safety of that habit was missing. Maybe it was in the trunk of the car. No matter, for tonight there was no way to communicate out of this deep remote canyon, not even cell phone service. I read for about an hour before falling asleep. The pillows were just right to prop me up for reading, but too fat for sleeping, so I got up to fold my fleece vest to use as a pillow. Once my eyes closed, I was out like a light!

Day 3

I slept long and hard. Sandy stirred about 7:30, and we decided to get up and see how our legs felt. No surprise, we were both a bit stiff, but things loosened up as we moved about. My legs were sore in the calves and around the hip joints. Otherwise, I seemed to be in good shape. We dressed and walked to the café. Both of us ordered oatmeal, but it was so thick we could hardly eat it. We talked again with the men from Georgia. One of them ordered a short stack of three pancakes. They were so huge, he offered us one, and given our disappointment with the oatmeal, we decided to accept his offer and split it between us. We made a good decision. It tasted great!

After breakfast, we went back to the room to pack for the day. We could carry much less this time, as it was a day trip. We would only be going three miles each way and the canyon is not so steep here. We stopped back by the office to check in and Sandy paid for both of us, as I had not found my wallet.

"Let's stop by the tribal office to see if we can use their phone," she suggested.

The clerk at the tribal office was kind and dialed for us, then handed me the phone, but the station attendant said nothing had been turned in.

We headed out of the village, deeper into the canyon. It was cool with a sharp wind, and I was glad I had brought my earmuffs along. They felt cozy and warm. The trail here was wider, perhaps five feet, with a soft sandy bottom, quite a contrast to yesterday, and the going was easier. The descent was gradual as we passed horses in corrals and came again to Havasu Creek. The trail followed the water and we stopped often for views and photos. The water was deep, maybe 15 to 20 feet, a brilliant turquoise blue and surprisingly warm. The average temperature is 70 degrees year-round. It is full of minerals, especially lime. The minerals are deposited on the streambed, with the carbonate precipitates creating tourmaline shelves, which appear like terraces along the bed of the stream. They build up so that the water falls over the terraces in small waterfalls. The smaller ones, called the Navajo Falls, were created this way. Over time, these terraces break away, creating a new surface for the streambed. These bright blue mineral terraces are what give the appearance of turquoise water.

We stopped as we crossed a bridge to look into the deep pools of crystal clear water. Ahead of us, we heard the roar of Havasu Falls before we actually reached it and, as we rounded the corner of the canyon, it came into full view. It was a breathtaking sight as the water cascaded, falling in a lacy pattern into a deep pool below, more beautiful than any picture could capture. The warm water vaporized to create a lovely mist around the falls, giving it an ethereal feel. Sometimes folks swim in the pools, enjoying the warm waters, but no one was there today. We took several photos and walked nearer the falls, following the stream as it left the waterfall pool and began to move down the canyon toward the campground. There were lovely scenic spots where the water pooled deeply, followed by areas where the travertine had built up deposits and the water cascaded over them.

We reached the campgrounds, easily distinguished by the composting toilets nearby. Inside the toilets were buckets of wood shavings. A sign asked you to add a scoop of the shavings saying, "Help us do our duty while you do yours." The toilets were clean, without odor, and certainly offered more comfort and privacy than the trips we took behind a rock as we came down the canyon yesterday.

We followed the stream slowly, walking downhill, admiring the water as we went, finally coming to Mooney Falls. This one dropped over 200 feet and was also beautiful, but not as stunning as Havasu Falls. The trail dropped sharply here as well, and the path was very narrow, stair-stepping steeply down and around the face of the cliff. I made my way down, holding on to the rock beside me for balance. There was a small chain as a kind of guardrail, offering a false sense of security. The footing was difficult, but I was finally able to reach a viewing area where I could see the entire length of the falls. The trail ahead was full of steep switchbacks and we decided we had gone far enough today on our weary legs.

We stopped for a leisurely lunch when we returned to the campground. The weather was pleasant and lingering near the stream relaxed us. Our respite over, we collected our things and continued back up the hill, soon coming again to Havasu Falls. Sandy had begun to pick out shapes in the rocks, noting a Mexican in a sombrero and a Koala bear. We took photos, but wondered if we would be able to identify the same shapes when we saw the pictures.

As we neared the village, men were digging a grave at the cemetery and we wondered who had died. A group of hikers came toward us heading down hill. They had a beautiful big yellow Labrador retriever that was carrying his own packs, one on each side.

While we were ordering dinner, the men from Georgia lined up behind us. We hiked the same trail today, except the men went a bit further into the canyon to the bottom of Mooney Falls. I felt that they genuinely admired us for participating in this rigorous adventure. They planned to head out in the morning at five a.m.! This was not for us, we thought. It isn't even light by then!

Day 4

We awoke at about seven a.m. and walked to breakfast. By mutual agreement from the previous day's experience, we ordered one order of hotcakes to share. We saw folks we met on the trail and exchanged stories of hiking yesterday as well as asking about other hikes, especially Bright Angel Trail and South Kaibab Trail. They are steeper and longer than the

Havasaupi Trail. Everyone was friendly and eager to share experiences. I told about hiking the Inca Trail to Machu Picchu last year and folks seemed envious.

Breakfast finished and packing completed, we dropped off our key in the box at the office. The weather was comfortable, a bit chilly, but with a bright clear sky that promised a good day for hiking. As we left the village, we noticed the stream on the right. On arrival two days ago, we were so tired that we barely noticed it. Today, the trail was wetter than when we came down and we found patches of mud and puddles of water to avoid. We noticed the birds calling loudly this morning. There were several varieties and the sounds of their various trills and warbles added a pleasant chorus to our adventure. The next two miles followed the stream then turned right as the canyon shifted in that direction. Now the terrain had a different character. It was definitely rockier, not soft dirt.

A pack train came up from behind, overtook us, and stopped just ahead. The packer dismounted and, starting at the end of his string of animals, one by one he untied their lead ropes from the horse in front and looped the rope over the packsaddle so it was off the ground. Once free, each animal began to walk independently up the canyon. The packer remounted and followed. We had stopped for a water break and a few minutes rest as we watched him, but now it was time to move on. The trail ascended more steeply and we cautiously watched where we put each foot as we walked. The stones and loose gravel made for an unpredictable surface. Suddenly, I heard Sandy slip and fall behind me.

She quickly said, "I'm OK!"

I urged her not to try to get up immediately but to collect herself first. I helped her take off her pack so she did not have to deal with that weight while trying to get back on her feet. Fortunately, she was not injured or even scraped. One of her hiking poles, however, did not fare so well. When trying to hold herself upright as her foot slipped on the gravel, most of her weight shifted to the left pole and it bent near the bottom.

She stated, matter-of-factly, "Well, better the pole than a hip!"

The pole was still usable and once we had her pack repositioned, we were ready to resume our trek. The group with the beautiful Labrador passed us. They would clearly be at the top far ahead of us. We exchanged greetings and they soon were out of sight.

Sandy was tiring, so we stopped for water. She wanted to keep moving, but I urged her to eat something to keep her energy up. We saw a woman working on trail maintenance, moving rocks with her gloved hands, and we stopped to talk. She said she was thrown from her horse yesterday and was a bit sore. She chose to work here today to move rocks, which had caused her horse to stumble. We noticed that the helicopter was making many trips today, and commented to the worker that the tribal dancers must be heading out to Fort McDowell for the PowWow. She said she had planned to go to the dance, but cancelled her plans because of a tragedy in the village. A young family from the village was in an auto accident near Wickenburg. Someone ran into their car. The mother and daughter were killed instantly; the father and son were in intensive care. We mentioned that we saw the workers digging graves yesterday. She said the village is in shock and mourning.

The woman asked where the other members of our group were.

I responded, "There's just us two old ladies."

"Oh," she said. "I hope I am in as good a shape as you are . . ."

Sandy and I smiled and Sandy finished her sentence, "When you are our age, right?"

The woman, embarrassed, nodded yes.

The day wore on and we kept an eye on the clock. There were hikers and pack trains coming and going. April is a popular month for this hike as it is still cool. The heat of the Arizona summer is not the time to be hiking the trails. We came upon the group with the Lab as they had stopped for lunch. One was from Flagstaff, one from Colorado, and one from Brazil.

At another point when we stopped, a passing group pointed out to us some ancient markings called petroglyphs, saying their guide showed them the spot. We were fortunate to have had the opportunity to see the ancient symbols, so in turn, pointed them out as two other groups came by. At last, we emerged from the narrower lower canyon and tramped across the wider valley floor approaching the base of the cliffs. It was much warmer here, as midday was approaching and we were in the broader canyon at a distance from the shade of the canyon walls. The trail steepened as we began to gain elevation, and there were at times steps to get over where railroad ties had been used to hold the soil in place.

Sandy lamented, "I'm not sure if I can make it."

I offered to trade packs with her as mine was a bit lighter, but she strongly resisted.

"Please don't do that," she said, "It's not fair!"

So I suggested a compromise. "I will agree to wait until we stop at the picnic area, but then we need to trade."

The trail was increasingly steep and rocky. We were moving, but slowly. It had been the plan to stop for lunch at the picnic area, but we were not there yet. We were tired and needed nourishment to boost our energy levels. We stopped where we were for lunch, water and a rest. As I looked up, I could glimpse the white storage containers at the trailhead, and pointed them out to Sandy. At least we could see our goal even if it was still over three miles away and several hundred feet above us. The food tasted good and the water was refreshing. We felt encouraged and energized.

"Now, it's time for us to exchange packs," I said.

Sandy protested.

"Your husband trusted your safety to me," I convinced her.

Though only a few pounds difference in the weight, changing packs would help her have less to carry. We assisted each other to put on our packs and trudged off again.

I watched as each footstep raised a small puff of dust. My boots were covered with a layer of red dirt. We gradually climbed another mile of rocky trail and arrived at the steep switchbacks. It was even slower going, with frequent rest stops, but we were making progress and could look back below us to view the elevation gain. A pack train was coming down the trail and I warned Sandy. Moving at this slow speed, we could not scramble, and needed plenty of time to find a safe place to get out of the way.

Every day, the tribe works to maintain the trail, which is heavily used by the pack animals as well as hikers. We estimated there were at least 200 horses, mules, and burros using the trail up and back daily. In an attempt to prevent erosion, the tribe has built walls about two feet high constructed along the outside of the trail to divert water from running down the trail. Sandy was exhausted and struggling to lift her feet even a few inches over rocks, but we moved to the side of the trail as the pack train came down. We were at the end of a switchback, well out of the path of the animals. On the trail near us, there was a small drop-off of about ten inches because of a rock in the trail. The animals eyed it as they chose their footing.

The Native American said to us as he rode by, "You would be safer if you waited on the other side of the wall."

Sandy sighed and out of his hearing said to me, "What he doesn't know is that I don't have the energy to get over that wall!"

Finally, we reached the last switchback and climbed out onto the parking lot. We felt like celebrating, but didn't have energy for the enthusiasm. We walked to the car, opened the trunk and began to pull off our packs and boots. I looked carefully in the trunk, shifting things around, hoping to find my wallet, but it was not there. Disappointed, I opened the car door to search inside and saw the wallet between the front seats. Tears flooded my eyes and I whispered a thankful prayer. I was so relieved! We got into the car and headed for home, about five hours away.

The next day . . .

Well, I am home safe and sound, though still a bit stiff in the calves of my legs. We had a wonderful trip, but the hike was strenuous. It took us seven-and-a-half hours to climb out the nine miles, with an elevation gain of 2,000 feet, much of that concentrated during the last two miles climbing up the side of the canyon. The brochure describes the hike as "very rugged terrain" and they aren't kidding.

I am unpacking and doing laundry. Mission accomplished! It is good to be home.

Navini Island, Fiji—A True Tropical Paradise

Bonnie Boyce-Wilson

A leisurely stopover on Navini Island in Fiji, to decompress following our busy travel itinerary in Australia, exceeded our fantasies of a tropical paradise. Fiji is a country made of over four hundred fifty islands in the warm, inviting waters of the South Pacific.

We landed in Nadi, the capital, after a three-hour plane trip from Sydney. We cleared Customs and were met by Henry, our driver. He took us to the dock area to board a small boat to Navini Island, where we were greeted and welcomed by staff who grabbed our bags and escorted us to our bure (one of ten beach cottages). The fully modern bure was prepared for our arrival with a personal note of welcome and a huge platter of fresh fruit.

Navini Island's best feature, along with golden beaches surrounded by crystal clear waters, is its Fijian people. The greatest pleasure of the island's thirty-two staff (who outnumber guests) was our enjoyment of the happiest, most relaxed holiday ever. The small island allows guests to experience a casual destination with the feeling of a private resort—indeed; the resort staff and guests are the only inhabitants.

Meals are included and served in an open dining room, decorated with lush tropical plants. We selected from a menu of fresh seafood, traditional and Fijian dishes. Everything is made on site in the kitchen, including fresh-baked breads and luscious desserts. One evening, we enjoyed a romantic candle-lit dinner on the beach, complemented by sipping from a freshly opened coconut.

At Navini, your time is your own for fishing, snorkeling, visiting other islands, and a variety of watercraft. We also participated in the afternoon beach volleyball games. Snorkeling was our greatest delight, as Fiji is home to the third largest coral reef in the world. The beach was only a few feet from our bure door, and we spent part of each day fascinated by the colorful fish, exotic corals, and the most amazing cobalt blue starfish. Our toughest decisions were whether to lie in the hammock by the bure or on a lounge chair under a thatched umbrella on the beach.

All too soon, our reverie ended, and we found ourselves back on the little boat headed for Nadi, forced to leave our daydream and awaken to the world of reality, vowing to return to Fiji.

If you go: Toll free booking number: 1-877-301-8772
Email: *naviniisland@connect.com.fj*

If I Could Be Anywhere

Judy Neigoff

If I could be anywhere in the world for a week, I would be back in Antarctica. I was there once in 1987, and it was unique—the most intense, awesome place I have ever been. We were on an expedition ship with a one hundred thirty other travelers plus a knowledgeable staff of naturalists and arctic experts. Though I know I'll probably never have a chance to return, I go there frequently in my mind.

No civilization exists in Antarctica. No people, busy streets or interesting buildings. No famous sights to see or fancy restaurants. No shopping! Instead, it is a place that just is. Quiet, ethereal, away.

Antarctica is white. It is unspoiled and timeless. Crystal icebergs in assorted fascinating shapes float gently on the rolling seas. You can nudge up to them in a Zodiac boat and chip away a chunk of the blue ice for your drink that night. As you circle an iceberg, it changes color and intensity as the light hits it from different angles. You play with its angles, shapes and colors all day and never tire of it. Like snowflakes, no two icebergs are alike.

The shores of Antarctica are rocky and icy. Sharp, glittery mountains soar up inland, peak after peak, as far as you can see. In summer, when we were there, the sun never sets but goes around in a circle, literally. The sun shines off the mountains and snow, almost blinding you. When stepping onto the shore, puffs of white snow catch the light and sparkle around you, magically. If the day is instead cloudy, the number of gray tones is amazing. We even had a snowy day, total whiteout with nothing but you surrounded by white, the whole continent seeming to disappear.

All this nothingness, and yet everything. If you know where to look, Antarctica is teeming with life. Our expedition ship brought us to the cliff where birds nest in the millions. The constant squawk is deafening.

And the constant motion of birds wheeling and soaring in the air currents overhead is dizzying.

Sea life is abundant even in these cold waters. Curious dolphins frolic beside the prow of the Zodiac. And Antarctica is the place where whales live when they are not traveling north to breed. Huge silvery shapes slide through the water, then suddenly surface with a whoosh of air from their blowholes. They arch and are gone.

But the best of Antarctica—the penguins! The funny little men in tuxedos who amused and enthralled us most of all. When our expedition staff took us to a penguin rookery, the sound and smell hit us first. Hundreds of thousands of penguins calling to their mates and waddling around in thick guano. We watched with smiles on our faces as they performed their love dances in pairs and built nests of small stones stolen from one another. The penguins didn't seem to mind the human audience, or perhaps they did, hamming up their antics to amuse us. They seemed to love getting their pictures taken, cocking their heads at jaunty angles or pecking their beaks against the camera lens.

I could, and did, sit whole afternoons watching penguins.

Taking a Back Seat

Greta Bryan

Riding stoker on a tandem bicycle for 400 miles allows a lot of time to rethink your 30-year-old marriage contract, the "honor and obey" part.

The guy in front is boss; he decides the direction, speed, cadence, braking, AND dares to spit into the wind. The stoker sits in back, pedaling her backsides off—with often a piece of tape slapped across her lips to mute obscenities and whining.

But it was worth giving up control to ride across miles of Belarussia and Russia along the same route the Nazi soldiers trampled and plundered, buried and bombed, in the early 1940s. We knew that if *they* could almost make it to Moscow in the dead of winter, uninvited, surely 12 Americans, paired on tandem bikes, accompanied by an American International Biking Tour guide, a Russian translator, and a Soviet police escort, could claim victory in the summer of 1988.

There were no group introductions until we met at the Warsaw airport, tired and rumpled. Had an English-speaking Pole not explained, "Bicycle-in-box-riding-to-Moscow" to a swing-shift Customs official, whose priorities did not include helping us, I'm doubtful we'd have made it out of the main terminal or found the three Polish taxi drivers waiting to haul our bodies and bikes 181 kilometers to the Polish border. Two bottles of vodka got us through Polish Customs, but it was a long wait at the Russian border. Our support van had to squat over a grease pit to allow an examination of its underparts. Continuing onward in the dead of night, our taxi driver was picked up for speeding and fined 2,000 ziloties, payable on the spot. We magnanimous Americans bailed him out by pooling three American dollars. *He* was impressed.

So what was it like biking in Russia? From bikers, that question means how were the showers and beds, food and water? The extras are good weather, decent roads, interesting people, and no flat tires. Russia scored a ten on the extras, a strong five on the basics.

Biking the quiet Moscow highway, built for the 1980 Olympics, reminded us of Iowa with a bit of northern Minnesota thrown in: rolling-to-flat roads bordered by wheat and cornfields and worked with farm implements reminiscent of the American 1940s. Well-padded women in faded print dresses, triangular scarves tied under their chins, and sweaters pulled taut over heavy bosoms worked alongside the men, raking, pitching hay, or sitting on a rock, milking cows.

Accommodations in local Russian hotels were clean, the beds hard, showers tepid, elevators scary. Toilets? The nose *always* knew before the eyes saw!

We were always hungry in spite of a daily overload of potatoes, bread, greasy gravied meat, and cabbage. *Lots* of cabbage. Riding stoker after a lunch heavy on cabbage is not recommended.

The basics, we groused or laughed about. But we were humbled by the people and their stories. There were few waves and smiles from the country roadside folks. Perhaps they had never seen an American OR a tandem bike but probably questioned the sanity of both. The shy young kids were the exception. They politely took turns riding the stoker seats and were a joy at every stop.

En route to Minsk, our one hundred-mile day, we stopped in a village for the trip's best meal. The napkins were obviously new, the price tag still dangling from the seam.

After lunch, I was approached by a Russian man who asked my age, so I told him.

He appeared shocked! "You should be home resting, and you are not big enough." He made cupped hand motions under his chest. (An obvious statement.)

In reply, I smiled, then swung my 34-inch inseam leg over the stoker seat and pedaled off.

Arriving at Minsk, site of the Communist Party's first meeting, we were met by seven Russian cyclists, who led us up the hilliest part of our ride, to Khatyn, once a town until Hitler's troops stormed it, corralled the people in a barn, torched it, then shot anyone who dared to escape.

We shared dinner that night, exchanged gifts, watched a slide show, and looked at Vladimir's gold medal he'd won racing in the 1976 Olympics.

During a question-and-answer session, we asked about the high rate of alcoholism. Vladimir shared that

Gorbachev really tried to sober up the Soviet Union by not allowing liquor stores to open until late afternoon. A sugar shortage mystery, following the announcement, was solved when the government realized the locals were using sugar to make their *own* hooch.

We changed police escorts at the border of each district. Peter, a gregarious New Yorker, decided that a thank-you gift was in order. Perhaps not politically correct but immensely appreciated, no doubt, he presented a six-pack of condoms to each driver. The throaty chuckles and untranslated comments undoubtedly spoke of future conquests! Our Russian guide, whose wife was pregnant, grinned, "Thank you . . . good later."

Riding the last ten miles, from the edge of Moscow into Red Square, was a heady experience. We biked in twos alongside six lanes of traffic. Throngs of people lined the streets, actually waving and smiling. A Soviet television cameraman, his head and camera hanging out of the car, filmed us while several bystanders tossed bouquets of flowers to stokers. We startled them by releasing both hands to accept the gifts. Little did they know—stokers can ride across America with no hands.

Processed film will keep the sights alive as will tape recorders the sounds, but we need neither to remember our Russian guide, Andrew, who rode most of the way on a bike provided by our American guide. Andrew could barely walk at the end of his first day. A unanimous vote decided the bike should be his to keep, a small tip in return for his sensitivity, infectious grin, sense of humor, intelligence, and candid conversations, which enlightened and delighted us each day. On our last day in Moscow, we passed an enormous outdoor swimming pool, which he reported was heated, full, and used all year. My husband, quickly sensing there was *no* water in the pool, asked why wasn't it working *that* day. Andrew replied simply, "Because it is this country."

And that's the way it is sometimes. It *is* because it *is*. Just ask a stoker.

FICTION

Two Pools for Pauline

Greta Manville

A small group of tourists followed the guide to the second floor of the Key West home where Ernest Hemingway lived during the 1930s with his second wife, Pauline. The young woman pointed to the unusual artifacts decorating the rooms as she explained their origins.

"Awesome," Kay murmured. "I'm an English major at NYU and Hemingway is my favorite author. I've read everything he wrote."

The members of the group nodded to acknowledge their interest too, then with quiet respect moved on to look around at the massive furniture, the sculptures, wall hangings, and delicate art objects collected on the author's trips to Europe and Africa.

"I wonder what it must have been like to be Ernest Hemingway when he lived here with Pauline, so long ago," Kay said as she lingered behind in the master bedroom. One of the tall window shutters had been pulled aside, allowing a view of the courtyard below. Kay slipped behind the tall shutter to stand before the open window. Gazing dreamily down onto courtyard, her attention was drawn to the sight of a large number of strolling or reclining cats. She hadn't noticed the cats when the group had hurried to enter the house. Now, she could hear a shrill voice coming from the courtyard below.

*   *   *

"Get that ugly thing out of here, and keep it out!" Pauline screamed from the kitchen, "I hate it! You know how I hate it!"

"Poor little Pussums," Ernest cooed to the six-toed, black-and-white cat, rigidly braced in his big arms. "Don't let Mama scare you."

37

Ernest walked down the steps to the courtyard. The morning sunshine felt warm and soothing after the icy blast from his wife. How a woman could get so ornery about a little cat drinking milk from her glass puzzled him. He decided the outburst might be from a slight hangover—or maybe brought on by the surprise he'd dragged home last night from Sloppy Joe's saloon.

"Mama shouldn't have left her glass of milk on the table, Pussums. She's always telling the children to mind their milk. She, of all people, knows better. Kitties think milk is for them." He kissed the top of the cat's silky head.

True, Ernest acknowledged, Pussums was ugly by standards of American shorthairs, her white face marred by a large inky blot extending from the nose to beneath her eyes. But it gave her character, even if it made her look like she'd dipped her face in an inkwell. "I should have named you Rorschach. Beauty isn't everything, Pussums. Look at me. I'm kind of homely, but I like to think I have other qualities people find attractive."

He set Pussums gently beside the porcelain object leaning against a palmetto at the side of the courtyard. "See what I brought you?"

Pussums walked off.

Ernest looked overhead at a dainty white cat draped among the branches of a banyan tree. "Look at this, Zelda. Know what it is?"

The cat stared disdainfully and washed her paw.

"Eleanor Roosevelt? Where are you? You'll appreciate this in time."

A longhaired, brown-and-white tabby brushed sensuously around Ernest's black boots, then she stood up and poked her head over the edge of the object.

"I knew you'd be interested. Where are the other girls?"

Ernest walked around to the side of the house. Picking up a metal pan, he banged his pocketknife against the bottom. "Come on, girls. Dinner time."

A half dozen cats jumped down out of the dense, spreading branches of trees overhanging the house and the high wall surrounding the property. A yellow, tiger-striped cat nudged her three multi-colored kittens from under the bushes.

Ernest grinned. "Sorry. Only kidding. I wanted to show off what Papa brought you for a surprise," he said, leading them to the center of the courtyard.

"A surprise all right," Pauline spat from the open doorway. "You can't be serious about installing that horrid thing in the front yard."

Ernest gave Pauline a long, cool assessment. "Pauline, all of my pussies drink a lot of water. You and the children have been woefully neglectful when I'm out of town, and this will solve the problem. I'll set it in concrete and install a running fountain. Then you won't have to worry about the kitties when I'm away. And I won't feel guilty about deserting my responsibilities."

"A urinal in my front yard? Ernest, you must be insane. What will our friends say?" Pauline stepped closer, scowling, but keeping a safe distance from the destested object.

"That you should have me committed, no doubt. Trust me, if you don't tell them, they won't recognize it when I get through fancifying it." He picked up a leopard-spotted kitten and tickled its ears. "You'll have to be careful not to fall in, little fellow. Maybe I should make a platform so the babies can get to the water safely."

"I thought you were drunk when you lugged that monstrosity into the yard last night."

"Be that as it may, the idea is a grand one."

"If you carry out this threat, I'm building a swimming pool in the back yard."

"Over my dead body. Do you have any idea what it would cost to dredge out the coral underneath this island to make a pool?"

Pauline laughed. "I thought money was no object."

"Think again then. I'm not made of money."

"And your last book didn't exactly win the Pulitzer. If you spent more time working and less on these damned cats, you might turn out something worthwhile."

Ernest thought about the short story he had completed earlier in the week. He called it "The Snows of Killimanjaro" and was rather pleased with the result. He'd assumed Pauline liked it, too. God knows, she'd liked Africa and wanted to go back.

"Pauline, the cats will have their watering hole."

"Ernest, I will have a swimming pool."

"No, you will not."

"Then it's me or the cats."

"Pauline, be reasonable." Pauline was always threatening to leave or throw him out. He was more worried about the swimming pool, which would bankrupt them. Maybe the urinal wasn't such a good idea after all.

"You are such an idiot, Ernest." Pauline turned back toward the house. "And you're wasting your talent. If you spent half as much time writing as you do picking off fleas and worming cats, we'd be rich." She slammed the front door after her.

"That does it." Ernest followed Pauline inside and climbed the stairs to the second floor, slowly, heavily weighing his decision. In the large bedroom, he picked up the telephone on his desk and looked up a number in the phone book. "Flagler 908," he said to the operator.

"Whitworth's," a voice answered.

"Bobby, I'll be over. I need some bags of cement and sand."

* * *

Snapping out of her reverie, Kay hastily rejoined the tour group, now strolling the courtyard.

"And this unusual looking fountain," the guide explained, "was created from a urinal Ernest Hemingway brought home from his favorite bar, Sloppy Joe's, which was being remodeled."

The urinal looked more like a shrine than a watering hole for cats. Set before a large Spanish olive jar, water poured into a trough, discreetly disguised by lush tropical flowers growing around and over its colorful tiles.

"Pauline added the tiles," the guide explained. "Now, more than forty cats, many descendents of Hemingway's six-toed cat, enjoy the author's foresight, though most, in truth, use the other outdoor fountains."

"Probably a matter of taste," Kay offered.

Cats of many hues and patterns lazed in the sun of the courtyard, stretched out around the courtyard or curled up on white wrought-iron chairs. Several peered between the stalks of tall ferns or from the branches of enormous banyans and pepper trees. Others strolled along the pathways in arrogant possession of their personal Garden of Eden.

"Follow me around to the right," the guide directed.

The group dutifully trailed after her.

"Pauline had a swimming pool built, much against her husband's wishes, it was rumored, while he was in Cuba fishing and writing. The pool was carved out of coral at tremendous expense." The guide pointed to the pool decking. "See this? It's a penny embedded in the concrete.

Hemingway is alleged to have said that Pauline might as well have his last cent, she'd spent all the rest, as he threw the coin into the wet cement."

What became of Pauline?" someone asked.

"The Hemingways divorced in 1940, and the Key West property went to Pauline until her death in 1951. In later years, Hemingway stayed here during his travels."

"So Pauline kept the cats—and the urinal?" Kay asked.

"The children urged her to keep the cats—"

"And Pauline kept the urinal to remind her why she and Ernest divorced." Kay's comment popped out before she could stop herself.

Everyone stared.

The guide laughed. "Time to move along."

The Question of Christmas
Judy Neigoff

"Ema (that is mother in Hebrew), what is Christmas?" asked five-year-old Avi. The family had recently moved to America from Israel and Avi was all questions about this new culture he found himself in.

"It must be an American holiday." Abba (father) answered. The government offices and banks are all closed that day, just like other American holidays. Some American holidays were easy to figure out, like the 4th of July, which is an Independence Day like Israel's Yom Ha'atzmaut or Thanksgiving, which came about when the Pilgrims read their Bible and patterned a harvest feast after the holiday of Sukkot described in the book of Leviticus. But he didn't know about Christmas. "I'll ask an American co-worker at the Embassy tomorrow about Christmas," Abba said.

The next evening, Abba had some answers for Avi. He said that he had found out that Christmas was the celebration of the birth of a man named Jesus who was born in Bethlehem.

"You mean our Bethlehem in Israel?" Avi shouted.

"Actually Bethlehem is in the Palestinian West Bank, but yes, there and not in the United States," Abba answered.

"Then was this Jesus a Jew or an Arab?" asked Avi.

"A Jew," answered Abba.

"Then Christmas is a birthday party for a Jew!" continued a delighted Avi. "And it's an American holiday so everyone celebrates it! What a great country."

Somehow Abba had trouble with this idea. When he thought about it, why would Americans celebrate a Jew's birth in Bethlehem? Abba decided that he would have to learn more about this holiday of Christmas.

At work the next day, Abba tried to inconspicuously observe what was being done to celebrate the Christmas holiday in America. He saw a secretary bring in a small fir tree and set it up on her desk. She opened a box and pulled out electric light bulbs that looked like candles and strung them around the tree.

"Look at my Christmas tree," she cried to anyone who walked by her desk.

"Americans celebrate Christmas by putting candle-like lights on trees," Abba told Avi that night.

"Then it is like Hanukkah, the Festival of Lights," said Avi.

Abba thought about that and again wondered if this could be true.

"But why would Americans put candles on trees instead of the Menorah?"

Abba had no answer for him.

But it seemed to be true. Everywhere Abba, Ema, and Avi went that next week, people in the community were putting up colored lights on lampposts, trees, and around their houses. The town was turning into a really pretty "Festival of Lights" indeed. They also saw, in front of a church, an artfully arranged set of statues with a mother and father wearing typical Middle Eastern robes gazing fondly at their new-born baby lying in some sort of wooden crib surrounded by the animals Avi used to see in his favorite petting zoo back in Israel: a camel, sheep and goats.

"Everyone is out buying Christmas presents," Ema reported the next day when she came home from shopping." A lady in the store said that she was going to wrap them in bright paper and put them under their Christmas tree. She said that her family opens them all on Christmas morning."

"I get presents for Hanukkah." said Avi. "And I get to open one each day for eight days. That sounds like more fun than just having it on one day."

Several days later, Abba, Ema, and Avi were just sitting down to dinner when they heard people coming up their front walk singing. Avi rushed to the window to see a choir right there in their front yard singing songs he had never heard before. After they had finished, Abba opened the door to thank the singers. Not knowing the customs and not wanting to offend, he invited them in for dinner.

"No, thank you," they called. "Merry Christmas." And off they went to sing at the next house.

Another strange custom that Ema and Avi observed as they went on chores about town was seeing several men dressed in the exact same type of red suit sporting a white beard. Some of these men were ringing bells along the sidewalk, one was sitting in a shopping center with a long line of children waiting to climb onto his lap, and one was even sitting in a sleigh at a car dealership holding a big white bag that had toy cars spilling out of it.

"Why do Americans do all these strange things to celebrate the birthday of the Jewish boy, Jesus, born in Bethlehem?" asked Avi at dinner one night toward the end of December. "And why is it so similar to Hanukkah?"

Abba wondered this himself. He realized that Jesus must have done something famous to have so many special celebration customs for his birthday. And he wondered if the timing of the holiday, around the same time of the year as Hanukkah, was on purpose or just a coincidence. He decided he had better do more investigation on the subject.

Asking around at work, Abba was referred to a local minister who was a friend of the secretary with the little Christmas tree on her desk. He talked to the minister on the telephone and ended up inviting him to dinner that night to share their Hanukkah celebration and to talk about Christmas. Luckily Ema, consulted after the fact, didn't mind putting on an extra plate for dinner. Avi was all excited at the prospect of talking personally to someone who actually celebrated this holiday of Christmas.

"So, who is Jesus?" Avi asked at dinner.

"He is the Son of God," replied the minister.

"Aren't we all children of God?" asked Avi.

"Out of the mouths of children," intoned the minister. "But Jesus is special. Sent by God, his true father, to walk here on Earth."

"I thought Joseph was his father. I saw the statues on the church lawn. Mary was his wife and Jesus was born in a barn with animals all around," Avi said.

"Not to be disrespectful," added Ema, "but if you believe God was really the father of Jesus, then he committed adultery with Mary as she was married to Joseph."

"Hold on." The minister flushed. "Let me straighten this all out. Mary was not married to Joseph at the time. An angel came to Mary and told her she would conceive God's son. It was an immaculate conception. Then she married Joseph."

Abba shook his head at all this. The God of Judaism that he was taught about couldn't go around having children! But for the sake of understanding this Christmas thing, he went along with the concept.

"Why was this Son of God born in Bethlehem in a barn?" he asked. "Surely God would do better for his own son."

The minister went on to explain how there was to be a great census in the land and Joseph and Mary traveled to Bethlehem, but the town was so crowded they could only find room in a barn, and Jesus was thus born in the manger.

"There is a problem with your story. The census was held in the spring in those days," Abba said.

The minister mumbled a bit and admitted that there was this slight discrepancy in the season of Jesus's birth, but it has been celebrated in December for centuries now.

"So why the Christmas tree?" asked Ema. "The fir tree is native to northern Europe and America and not ancient Israel."

Again the minister mumbled a bit, then talked about the traditions of decorating Christmas trees, caroling, and telling the story of Santa Claus.

"I don't believe that chimney thing," said Avi, although he was entranced by the story. "And if it were like that, how does Santa Claus know which chimneys are Jewish or Arab ones so he doesn't need to come down those?"

The minister, feeling quite frustrated, pointed out that it was getting late. He added that he enjoyed watching the family light the Hanukkah Menorah, eating the potato latkes that Ema served with dinner, and playing driedel with Avi. He left saying that he hoped the family would find it in their hearts to accept Jesus some day and celebrate Christmas.

After Avi went to bed that night, Abba and Ema talked quietly together about all that they had learned about this question of Christmas. It was not at all connected to Hanukkah, a celebration of the Jewish people uniting under Judah Maccabee to drive out the occupying Assyrian-Greek forces, then rededicating the Temple in Jerusalem to Judaism, all of which took place one hundred sixty-four years before the birth of Jesus. And it was not a Jewish concept to worship a human, even if he claimed to be the Son of God. So they went to bed agreeing that they would tell Avi that although most Americans celebrated Christmas, Christmas was not for their family.

"That's OK," said Avi, the next morning. "I just wanted to know what Christmas was."

One Day of Dying

Joan Fedor

Rena opened her eyes in the new, quick, startled way. She tried to remember what it was like to struggle awake, to fight drowsiness, to grapple with the alarm in stunned indignation, to linger in the relaxed shadow of half-awareness. Now she moved from oblivion to instant perception with an overwhelming suddenness.

She lay flat to breathe slowly and deeply, determined to gather calm for the long day of coping. But as in other mornings of the past month, this intake of early stillness merely aroused the panic that stretched like an unborn child below her heart and in the visceral cavity of her abdomen. She could feel it brazenly ripple the corridor where desire lived and push impudently against her bladder creating a tremor of childlike urgency. She closed her eyes tight against the silent screams this powerful fetus sent along the veins of her skin and marshaled behind the hardness of her eyes. She felt full to the brim with this burden of truth.

Quickly she sat up and stared into the mirror beyond the bed, as though expecting eruptions of hysteria to rise like giant boils across the smoothness of her face and neck and arms. How could that image of stillness, its mouth closed, its head erect and arms unflailing be the host of fear and despair? There was no reality in that stick-like rumpled woman who stared back at her. She was a caricature of all the wives of the world rising to the routine of life.

Rena turned away from the mirror's flat reflection. She looked across the room to the ornate crucifix that hung beside the bedroom door—a burnished body against dark wood. She pulled back the soft blankets and knelt beside the bed. The familiar words seemed strange against the turmoil of her mind. "Oh my God, through the Immaculate Heart of Mary, I offer you my prayers, works, and sufferings of this day . . ." She could not continue the routine petitions of the prayer. For a moment she studied the crucifix and tried to see a dying man beneath the gold veneer. For the first time she needed to understand the indignity of suffering. She needed to believe that the mind, the spirit, the soul could withstand the terrible desolation of the body. She closed her eyes and whispered, "Help me, help me." Then she rose and crept softly past her husband's bed. She could not look at him while he slept—not yet.

The living room was cool and dark. Rena went to the large front window and opened the heavy curtains. High in the east—above the wooded ravine—the summer sun swept the ocean fog inland to disappear like giant balls of thistle in the surrounding hills. Solid robins hopped flat-footed across the wet gray grass and glistening rhododendrons trembled in the early breeze. The fragile leaves of the silk tree below the window unfurled in the promise of the distant sun. Rena closed the curtains against the glory of the day.

In the kitchen she sipped cold pungent juice while the coffee pot sent a lush aroma through the room. She watched the eruptions in the glass knob of the percolator darken, then she filled a cup. The coffee was strong and soothing: it softened the raw edges of fear. She pressed her cold hands against the hot mug and drank slowly. She didn't hear Lloyd until he stood at the kitchen door.

He said, "Coffee smells good."

"Oh, did I wake you?" She jumped up surprised and confused.

"No, no, sit down." He avoided her eyes.

Rena bit the inside of her bottom lip and hesitated. Then she said, "Did you sleep all right?" God, she hated these hollow morning conversations.

"Yes, I didn't wake up at all. Those are pretty good pills." He sat down suddenly.

Rena watched his eyes open wide—beads of perspiration showed above the startled lines of his forehead. She reached her hand across the table to touch him, but he jerked away.

He snarled through clenched teeth, "Give me some coffee."

Her hand shook as she poured the coffee. She put the cup in front of him and turned back to the stove.

"Rena!" He said her name in a furious command.

"It's too early for a pill. You know what the doctor said . . ."

He pushed the chair away from the table, banging it against the wall. His cup tipped and hot coffee spilled across the table and onto the floor.

"Oh, look what you've done," she complained. "And I just waxed the floor." She looked at him quickly, her words still hanging in the air. His expression was wild, bewildered and afraid. "I'm sorry," she said lamely, while panic screamed through her chest.

He stood up slowly—waited for a minute—then supporting himself against the wall went back to the bedroom.

As she watched, she said to herself, "It's too early to cry . . . It's too early to cry . . . It's too early to cry . . ."

She went down to the basement laundry room and filled a bucket with warm water. Picking up a sponge mop, she went back to the kitchen and the soiled floor. She cleaned up the coffee, then washed the rest of the linoleum. Her nightgown and robe hung heavily around her legs—her clothes were in the bedroom.

When she finished, she poured the cloudy water from the bucket into the wooden plant box on the back patio. The tree fuchsia in the box drooped with a profusion of scarlet dangling blossoms. She clipped some of the graceful flowers. They could float in the crystal bowl. She would put them on the nightstand between their beds. She took the flowers into the house and arranged them carefully: the petals turned limp and brown if over-handled.

After the flowers were ready and the bucket and mop were back in the laundry room cupboard, she looked at the clock and thought, "Why does the time go so slowly?" Though she knew the quarter-hours before pills dragged and those after rushed by. Finally it was time.

She filled a small glass with orange juice and shook out one of the red capsules from the bottle labeled: "Lloyd Walton. One every four hours for the relief of pain." She went into the bedroom and said, "Here is your juice. I'll bring some coffee in a minute."

He lay on his side with his face to the wall.

"Lloyd, do you need help?"

He shook his head slowly.

She went back to the kitchen and prepared a tray—a bowl of cereal, milk, coffee, a sweet roll. Usually, she ate most of it. She listened to him splash in the bathroom sink. When he returned to the bedroom she went in. He was sitting up in bed. His face was pale and clean, his hair smoothly combed, and he smelled of shaving lotion. She put the tray across his knees and sat on the chair beside his bed.

"Lloyd, let me bring you a basin and wash cloth. You don't need to get up."

"I might spill it all over the bed and myself. Then you'd have to clean it up."

Of course, I deserved that. Rena smiled and said lightly, "Oh, I'll take that chance."

"No, I don't want to inconvenience you." He looked grim and petulant and vulnerable. "I know I'm getting careless."

"You look very nice and you smell good." She loved him so much. She moved to kiss his cheek.

He pulled away. "Don't baby me, Rena."

"All right, Lloyd. How about some cereal?"

"Some coffee first." She saw him shudder helplessly at the solid food.

"OK, here you go." She poured the coffee.

He lifted it to his lips and sipped slowly. "Ugh! It's too strong. You always did have trouble making coffee."

"Please don't be unfair, Lloyd . . . I need you."

"Oh, God, Rena, what's unfair? You don't need me. You'll be fine. The house will be paid for. Just remember to watch the car . . . change the oil . . . get it greased . . ." He put his head back on the pillow and closed his eyes.

"Lloyd." She wanted to lie down beside him and hold on.

"Please Rena, turn on the radio and take this damn tray and get out." He didn't look at her.

She picked up the tray and went back to the kitchen. While she washed the dishes, she realized that she still wasn't dressed. When the doctor told them how hopelessly sick Lloyd was, she decided to stay with him in the bedroom. Now she thought it would be better if it weren't necessary to go in there for so many trivial things. But it was too late to change anything.

She took the crystal bowl of fuchsias back into the bedroom. Lloyd lay quietly listening to the radio. He didn't open his eyes when she put the flowers beside the bed. She took her clothes from the closet and went into the bathroom to dress.

He weathered the period before the noon pill and even finished a bowl of chicken soup for lunch. After they ate, Rena sat beside the bed and knitted, but he didn't speak to her. When he fell asleep, she left the room.

Late in the afternoon, she heard him scream her name. She ran into the bedroom. He was lying on his back clutching the bedposts above his head. His face was leaden and shining with perspiration.

When he saw her, he groaned through clinched teeth, "I want to go to the hospital."

"Lloyd, it's just that you slept through a pill."

"Damn you," he cried, "you don't care about me."

"I'll get a pill."

She rushed from the room as he shouted, "Oh, goddamn you . . . goddamn you."

She brought back the water and capsule and held his shoulder while he drank. As he lay back panting, he whispered, "Get out of my sight."

Rena warmed more chicken soup and left it on the stove. She made herself tea and took it into the living room. She turned on the television and as the dinner round of talk shows and news commentators flicked by, she cried. Tomorrow, she would call Dr. Shelton. Maybe the dosage should be increased . . . he should go the hospital? What good was she doing him? She felt limp and numb.

After a while, Lloyd came and sat heavily beside her.

She was afraid. "What are you doing up? Please go back to bed."

"I wanted to see the playoff scores." He smiled weakly. "Are our guys hanging in?"

"Lloyd?"

He leaned back wearily. He reached out his hand to her. She held the thin, wasted fingers.

"Rena, I love you."

"It's all right, Lloyd."

"But I am so sick, I don't know what to do. I try to pray, but everything seems so different . . . don't hate me."

Rena put her head on his shoulder. His arm lay heavy across her back. She reached across his body and pressed close to him. There were still two more hours before the next pill.

Baucis and Philomen *redux*

Greta Manville

Isabel stood before the tattered screen door, staring at the reddish-gold dog hairs snagged in the loosened wire and splintered wood. From the layered grime surrounding the doorknob, she could see that others had reached out eons before she found this convenience store set in hell. Reluctant to enter but pressed by her limited options, she took a deep breath, then added her own sweaty palm prints to the amalgam of recorded visitors.

$*$ $*$ $*$

The day had started well enough, with coffee and a free continental breakfast at the cheerful, hospitable Utah motel just short of the Arizona border. She relished the drive home after visiting her daughter Cindy, a literature professor at the state university in Logan. Isabel had made the trip many times and always returned from the visits to Cindy and her three children with mixed feelings: pleased by accomplishing her motherly visit, but relieved to part from Cindy's and Ted's unruly little brats. She wondered where she'd gone wrong rearing Cindy that she could bring up such undisciplined, graceless children. And Ted, a professor of chemistry deep into research, was no help.

The roads were not crowded, the morning bright and clean with the sparkling beauty of the Arizona desert. By late morning, the temperature had climbed to fifteen degrees over one hundred as she descended from the northern plateau toward the Valley of the Sun. Isabel blessed the car's air conditioning that allowed her to enjoy the scenery while protecting her from the blistering heat.

Eager to reach home, she decided to take a shortcut she'd driven several times in the past. It would cut off at least ten miles. She looked forward to getting back to her familiar routine of golf and bridge and hospital auxiliary work. She deeply missed her husband since his death three years ago but found a measure of contentment in a well-ordered life filled with pleasant friends and comfortable activities.

Without warning, the car coughed, sputtered, and died, abandoning Isabel a remote forty miles from home. She cursed herself for leaving the Interstate to take the shortcut. After her initial anger subsided, she reached for her cell phone to call Triple A.

"Great! The #$% thing is dead!" She tried the phone charger but it showed no sign of life either.

Panic set in as she realized there were few ranches and fewer gas pumps along the route. Her car was only a year old, serviced as the manufacturer required, and trouble-free until now. Still under warranty, but what good would a warranty do if she were found dead from heatstroke?

Isabel had seen a couple of other motorists on the cutoff, so surely someone would come by to help. As she stepped from the car, she hesitated. Could she trust anyone who stopped to offer assistance? They might rob her—or worse.

She paced for a couple of minutes, then returned to the car to sit with the doors open. Without a breeze, the heat quickly built up inside the car. An annoying insect buzzed around her head, warily escaped her swatting hands.

Isabel waited for thirty minutes, praying a heaven-sent highway patrolman or a Triple A tow truck would show up, but only two pickups passed without slowing down. With the August sun turning her car into an oven, she summoned up courage and began to walk. She had a faint sense that some sort of gas station or convenience store was a few miles down the road. Carrying only her purse and a plastic bottle of water, now half empty, Isabel headed toward whatever help she could find.

The soft purples and mauves of the desert scenery, so striking from her air-conditioned car, quickly turned into a scorched landscape designed by Satan. Isabel's feet began to swell, making every pebble on the road feel like a craggy boulder. She sipped the water until it was gone. Her perspiration dried as fast as it hit the hot, dry air, and she soon began to feel light-headed. She tried to jog, but could scarcely catch her breath. Her ankles, always weak, turned easily, and she tripped, sprawling onto the dirt and gravel alongside the road. Her sunglasses flew onto a rock, breaking the frame in half.

The only thing lacking to complete her journey through perdition was a rattlesnake, a thought that made her scramble to her feet. Isabel dusted off her slacks, determined not to let this silly incident get the best of her. Squinting down the road, she rejoiced at the sight of a shimmering low building not more than two hundred yards away. It must be the convenience store she remembered. She hadn't seen it before she fell, but then she'd been concentrating on keeping her footing.

$$* \quad * \quad *$$

Isabel turned the doorknob gingerly and stepped inside the store. As she waited for her eyes to adjust to the darkened room, cool air circulated by an overhead fan revived her spirits.

"He'p you, ma'am?" A burly, bewhiskered little old man spoke up from behind the counter.

Isabel looked around. The large room had shelves lining the wall, but most shelves were empty. A few held cotton bags, heaped in no particular order. Some spilled their contents, meal or beans, allowing cockroaches to play in their treasure trove. Cobwebs hung from the blades of the fan and from the corners of the room.

A slight cough to her left caused Isabel to look over her shoulder. Part of the room was cleared for living quarters in a shabby but functional decor that might have been inspired by the cartoonist George Booth. A light bulb hung by a cord from the ceiling, a tall philodendron leaned in front of a side window where a skinny yellow cat stood in the clay pot nibbling the plant's leaves. An old lady sat in a rocker toiling at some kind of handiwork, while a moth-eaten golden retriever lay at her feet watching the cat. The cat jumped down from the potted plant, kicked the fleas behind its ears, and threw up on the floor. The dog dutifully hoisted itself to its feet, groaned, and licked up the mess.

"Ma'am?" the old man asked again.

"Uh," Isabel returned her attention to the man behind the counter. "I guess you're not open for business."

"What give you that idea?"

"You seem . . . never mind. I wonder if I could use your phone."

"Sorry, don't have one."

"No phone?"

"Don't need one. We get deliveries regular."

Isabel looked at the nearly empty shelves. "But, what if you're sick or something?"

"Never git sick."

Isabel glanced at the old woman.

As though reading her mind, the old man said, "Lindy don't never git sick neither. The dog and cat, well, they take care'a theirselves."

Isabel sunk her hands impatiently into the pockets of her slacks. "I've had car trouble, a few miles up the road."

"Not surprised. Pretty bad road."

The old man sounded sympathetic. His bright blue eyes looked intelligent and kind, but Isabel couldn't figure out why he stood there, calm in the face of her monumental crisis.

"I need help." Her voice wavered as she thought of the long, hot trip by foot and how sore her feet were now. "May I sit down for a few minutes?"

"Sure, now I'm fergittin' my manners. We don't git many visitors."

"But this is a store, isn't it?"

"Most'a the stuff on the shelves, we use ourselves. My name's Wood, Phil Wood, and this is my wife Lindy. Lindy, come over here and make this lady to home."

The old woman rose stiffly from the rocker and walked over to peer at Isabel through smudged glasses. "I can't see too well," she apologized, "but I can tell you're a mite sunburned. Whyn't you set down, an' I'll fix you some lemonade."

"You needn't go to the trouble," Isabel said, "but I would appreciate a glass of water."

"Shouldn't travel in the desert without a supply of water," the old man chastised.

"I had water, but I drank it getting here." Isabel didn't know why she should have to defend herself to this stranger, but he made her feel like a retarded child.

"You set," the old woman said, "an' I'll be right back."

Bypassing the wet spot on the floor left by the dog's tongue, Isabel politely left the rocker for her hostess and sat primly on a studio couch under the front window. The musty-smelling couch was covered by a faded, hand-sewn quilt and animal hair. Though threatened with a high colonic from the coil of a spring poking through the quilt, Isabel stoically refused to show her discomfort, easing instead to another position straddling a less lethal spring.

The old woman went into what appeared to be a restroom at the rear of the store. "Now, Butterball, don't drink outa the toilet," Isabel heard the old woman say in a gentle, coaxing voice. "That's a bad kitty. Scoot."

The cat streaked out of the room and across the open expanse of floor, disappearing behind the counter where the old man seemed preoccupied with adding up receipts.

"Umph," he groused, "too many folks don't want to pay their debts."

Lindy returned with a glass of water. Her smile was sweet, if somewhat toothless, and it occurred to Isabel that the woman must have been pretty when she was young. The old man wasn't too bad looking either, just grizzled and rumpled.

Lindy held out a plastic bottle of water. "This isn't cold. You know how Arizona pipes are in the summer, but it's wet."

"Thanks." Isabel accepted the smeary, unsealed bottle. Though her mouth felt parched and dry, she hesitated to take a drink, weighing the possibilities of salmonella or ptomaine poisoning, maybe the bubonic plague, against the certainty of dehydration.

"It's all right," the old woman said, watching her. "I washed out the bottle. Aren't you thirsty?"

Isabel uncapped the bottle and took a quick sip. The water tasted rusty. "Well water?" She hoped the well wasn't downhill from a septic tank.

"Yes," Lindy smiled. "Good, pure well water."

The old man looked up from his paperwork. "I guess you'd like me to look at your car, see if I can fix it."

Isabel sighed with resignation. "I would, but in this heat, I couldn't ask you to go out and work on my car. Could we maybe flag someone down on the road and ask them to call Triple A for me?"

"Better, I could hitch it to my pickup and bring it in the yard here. I'm a whiz with fixin' cars, but it'd be easier working under the shade'a that big tree."

Isabel looked out at the lone tree standing in the middle of the gravel yard. Its thick-leaved, spreading branches created a dark, welcome respite from the punishing sun.

"What a beautiful tree," she said. "Unusual for the desert."

"It's a big, old oak. We planted it a long time ago," the old man said with pride. He and Lindy exchanged smiles. "Ten degrees cooler under there."

"Better'n that, Phil," Lindy chimed in. "I can hang wet wash from its branches an' it's dry in fifteen minutes on a day like this." Her voice trilled in a girlish way that made her sound a little simple-minded.

The old man put his arm over his wife's shoulders and grinned. "She sure can do wonders around here."

Lindy smiled up at her husband and picked a chunk of egg yolk from his whiskers. "Reminds me, I'll bet you're hungry," she said to Isabel. "While Pa goes for your car, whyn't I fix you something to eat?"

"No, no. I'm not hungry, really. I had a huge breakfast." Isabel hoped her stomach wouldn't betray her by growling while she thought of food, but the last thing she wanted was to consume any food from this household.

"Suit yourself. I'll go back to my handiwork, if you don't mind. Whyn't you take a little nap. Bein' out in this heat's hard on a person."

"I'll just sit here, thanks. I really appreciate your husband's help.

Isabel returned to the couch and found an acceptably safe niche to sit on. While she waited, she studied the huge oak tree, pondering how it could possibly survive, even thrive, in such arid country. Maybe a natural spring down deep fed its roots, but still it was a wonder. In the heat of the day, no birds flew among its branches, but surely in the spring the thick leaves protected nests of young birds from the desert predators.

Before long, Phil drove into the yard, towing Isabel's car to a shady spot beneath the tree. He set about his business working under the hood, and soon Isabel heard her car's engine start.

Phil came in the front door, the only door, wiping the sweat from his face with an oily rag. "All fixed," he beamed.

Isabel ran to him and shook his hand. "Oh, thank you, thank you. How can I ever repay you?"

Phil smiled but said nothing. He looked over at Lindy, who ducked her head, concealing a secret smile.

"What do I owe you? Did you have to use a new part? Whatever it is, I'll pay it. I have a credit card if I don't have enough cash."

"You don't owe us nuthin'."

"But I do. I can't let you work so hard without compensation. At the very least, I can make up for some of those bad debts you were fretting over."

Phil took her hand in his greasy paws and patted it gently. "You can do a good deed for another troubled person some day. That's all the pay I need, little lady."

"I don't believe this. It's unreal! You've saved my life, and you won't even let me pay for the auto repairs." Isabel verged on tears. "It's been a long time since anyone performed *any* kind of a service for me without charging an arm and a leg."

"Oh, well, be careful. We might just take an arm and a leg, mightn't we, Lindy?" The merry look in the old man's eyes told Isabel he was teasing. "We don't have much use for money. Put your credit card away. We got everything we need."

"I guess you do at that," Isabel conceded. "You know something? I envy you."

The old couple stood in the yard wrapped in one another's embrace. They waved as Isabel went on her way. Warmed by their charity, she told herself she would do something special for them when she next passed by.

*   *   *

The following spring, Isabel headed toward Utah to share her grandchildren's Easter break. All winter, she had worked on a quilt to give to the old couple. They could definitely use a clean one. She'd never quilted, but she took lessons and carefully designed a pattern with two people sitting under a spreading oak tree with their cat and dog.

As she neared the location of the store, she spotted the oak tree and became excited as she thought of the pleasure she would bring to these good people. But something was wrong. Where was the store? The tree was there, in the gravel yard, but no store, only a foundation of charred remains.

Isabel stopped the car and walked toward the tree. Twined around its trunk was a young sapling, small-leafed but already strong.

I knew it, she thought. An artesian spring must be below ground. These trees couldn't grow without water. The younger tree must have sprung up since I was here last, appearing almost to sprout from the trunk of the old tree. If only the trees could talk and tell me where the old couple has gone.

She started to leave, then remembered her gift. She took the quilt from her car and hung it from the branches of the oak tree.

"Maybe some poor soul will stagger along this road as I did," she said to the oak, "seeking respite from the sun or protection from cold winter air. I'll leave this and hope somehow to repay my debt."

Isabel returned to the car and slowly drove on her way, sad, but enriched by the knowledge that the old couple's goodness transcended their temporal shortcomings. Their generosity was an example she would carry to her grandchildren. Isabel smiled as she thought of the challenge ahead and hurried on her way.

POETRY

The Anasazi

Anne Levig

They say that Those Who Came Before have gone.
The Ancient Ones have left without a trace.
They dwelled high up in cliffs and caves of stone,
So safe from foe in well protected space.
For years they lived on arid lands so vast,
Where days grew warm and skies were often blue.
But have they truly gone, these Ancients past?
Have whistling winds erased them from our view?
Ah, no. They left behind their mark on clay.
Their etchings carved reveal details of life:
Their gods, their sun and moon, and birds of prey,
Their rainbow sign, their work with spear and knife.
      Their walls can talk, and much they have to tell
      With pictographs that tell their story well.

A Certain Honeysuckle

Joan Fedor

The hovering cold brittles bare
Stems and mottles hard leaves
From green to deep wine.

A dry maze of tendrils climb
The fence weaving a mound
Of clumped gauche lines.

In the under layer of twisted
Briar, bent stiff twigs
Open yellow slits.

The honeysuckle secretly
Sprouts in the thick gray
Of winter's noon.

Before crocus colors soften
The ground its gangling
Wood flushes green.

Pale gold blossoms like finely
Curved filament pique
New summer sun.

Hummingbirds skim dull silver
Over gilt blooms and
Red shining berries.

A slack moon blacks the night
Clogging the air with dew and
Dull heavy gloom.

Across the wet and dark the
Sweet smell of honeysuckle
Starts to grow.

Through the deep blind the sudden
Scent rises honeyed soft
And richly wild.

Blunt senses flair
To aromatic life in
The sightless sleeping night

Arizona Haiku

Mary Graham Bond

Aspen trees loosen
Their fluttering cloaks of gold—
Arizona fall.

Monsoon's wild storm strikes!
Now the streambed's dusty throat
Finds its river voice.

Small jaunty beetle
Climbs on spider-web staircase—
Gauzy entrapment.

The Immigrant

Ethel McNaughton

When first we meet . . .
"I love your brogue
Tell me your tales!
Is it Scotland?—England—Ireland—Wales?"

I answer . . .
"All of the above, and many more . . .
Always seeking at each new shore . . .
A short sojourn at first . . . then longer stays,
It seems I've been in AMERICA all my days . . .

Across oceans wide . . . and back again
I dream of hills, and misty glens
And the Pipes that call again and again . . .

It is hard to discard . . . the brogue rolls clear,
It is peace and contentment now that is dear
I gave up the crown and the cross of blue
To adopt America's red, white and blue . . ."

History has shown . . .
"ALL people seek freedom from oppression and slavery
And absentee landlords . . . that put down bravery
. . .who steal the sweat of your brow and shackle the soul
And kill those who do not pay the toll . . .

To answer the call that comes again and again
Of Freedom and those who yearn to be free . . .

I am home . . ."

Haiku

Mary Graham Bond

Hanging from the eaves
Morning icicles like swords
Guard sleeping children.

Alone in cold woods.
Trinket snow falls on small pines.
Above, buried stars.

Found in opera coat
set aside for discarding . . .
small, hidden pocket

Seeing Niagara . . .
Little girl exclaims:
"Wow! Did they MAKE this?"

Contraditty

Virginia McElroy

"I don't want to be catty, but her hair's a mess."
"I don't want to be frank, but
      I don't like your dress."

"I don't want to be nosy, but what did it cost?"
"I don't want to be crude, but
      I wish you'd get lost!"

"I don't want to be bossy, but do this my way."
"I don't want to be cheap, but
      It's your turn to pay."

"I don't want to brag, but I make better jam."
"I don't want to be rude, but
      I am."

You See . . . I'd Never Before Been a Grandmother

Greta Bryan

When I first saw you . . .
   asleep . . . in your cradle
   at the foot
   of your mom and dad's bed . . .

So very small . . .
   hands clutched under your chin . . .
   An unexpected rush of love left
   me weak
   and speechless.

As I looked down at you
   in awe and amazement . . .
   the memory of holding your precious
   mother for the first time . . .
   many years ago
    filled my heart.

BUT THEN, I'D NEVER BEFORE BEEN A
GRANDMOTHER

During those first few days of your life
    I slept in the room
    next to yours . . .
    one ear always open . . .
    waiting for you to wake up.

I couldn't believe that at the
    first wee cry
I rolled off the fouton with such
    ease, energy
    and enthusiasm . . .
    even in the middle of the night
      or very early in the morning!

I looked forward to those sounds.

I JUST COULDN'T BELIEVE THAT I WAS YOUR
    GRANDMOTHER

How I loved holding you close
    wrapped in your new soft blanket . . .

Together we slipped downstairs
    and into the kitchen
    warmed your bottle of mom's milk,
    then nestled into the rocking chair . . .
    and looked out into the night
    hopefully without waking your mama
      who needed her rest
    or your daddy
      who was trying very hard to get the
      hang of being a daddy.

And now, as I think back over
 your first year of life . . .
I realize that you are
 never far from my thoughts.

I can still see your smile,
 the creases at your wrists,
 the blue of your eyes
 the way your hair stuck up
 in the morning
 the feel of your skin . . .
I can see the way you
 climbed stairs and slid down backwards
 your pointer finger that loved to push
 buttons on the phone
I sense your devotion to your mother . . .
 never wanting her to get too
 far away . . .

I smile, remembering your
 excitement when friends came to visit . . .

Do you know that
 I talk to you each day?
 I look at your pictures stuck on my cupboards, bulletin
board . . . in my purse . . . on my desk at work.
And I say . . . "Hi Adam . . . how are you today?"
 (sometimes I even kiss your picture when
 no one is looking).

NO ONE TOLD ME THAT BEING A GRANDMOTHER
WOULD BE SO EMOTIONAL!

We're learning
   you and I.
I know that I must
   not worry about
      what you eat for breakfast or
      if your ears are covered when you
         are out in the wind . . .
      or if your hands
         get washed before you eat
      or if a stranger gets too close
         to you and
            breathes in your face . . .
I have to practice not to
   be bossy
I have to have talks
   with myself.
I say, "Now, Greta, Adam is NOT your son . . .
   you need to abide by
   the Adam rules."

You're learning how to be a
   big person
and I'm learning
   how to be a grandmother.
God knows a lot
   about you . . .
He knows about your broken leg
   and your surgeries and
   when your nose is running
   and your ears are hurting
   and when your gums hurt in your mouth.

GRANDMOTHERS NEED TO KNOW
   GOD IS CLOSE TO THEIR
   GRANDCHILDREN

I knew BEFORE you were born that
   I would love you, but
   I never could have imagined
   how MUCH . . .

BUT THEN, I'D NEVER BEFORE BEEN A GRANDMOTHER!

Capsule Comment

Virginia McElroy

Some for sleeping
Some for waking,
Some for headaches in the making,
Some for doldrums,
Some for tension,
Some for sinus-cold prevention,
Some for babies,
Some for none,
Some for trips *ad nauseum*,
Today I saw the druggist's bill—
And ran to take another pill.

Pentecostal Movement 1969

Joan Fedor

Lavern Beck has the gift of tongues.
All that jogging produced the change
That comes through his turtle neck out of his lungs.

And curls the toes stripped in leather thongs
Of Mrs. Beck chanting over her range,
Lavern Beck has the gift of tongues.

She praises the miracle as the work of hymns,
Hearing Luther and John in the sacred rage
That comes from his turtle neck out of his lungs.

But his churchly views are modest ones,
Nixon, Warhol, and Mailer more presage,
Lavern Beck has the gift of tongues.

And on that dread day when he succumbs
To the clogged corroded sounds of age
That comes through his turtle neck out of his lungs,

Autopsy will show fat from his veins,
Pumped to his brain, prompted the reportage,
Lavern Beck has the gift of tongues
That comes from his turtle neck out of his lungs.

Passage

Greta Manville

Weightless,
I float alone through the dark house,
my girth of years shed by this day's discovery
of the killer gnawing
within.

Sightless,
no moon-illumined shadows cast out
darkness to reveal well-loved possessions,
but I know each object
by heart.

Mindless,
I begin to count, not missed joys, only
missed sorrows, deaths I shall never need to grieve,
the cruel years of aging,
all gone.

Hopeless?
No, strangely I feel young again,
curious and unafraid to find what lies ahead,
over which I have
no control.

First published as the Grand Prize winner Sparrowgrass Poetry Forum's *Poetic Voices of America*, Spring 1999

REMEMBERING

A Sight to Behold

Greta Bryan

All his face revealed under the surgical drape was an unmoving left eye, blinded for twenty years by a dense cataract. Now it resembled a white opaque marble held stationary by local anesthesia. Though he didn't show any emotion, Amandu was undoubtedly scared, fearing what many African patients fear . . . that the doctor was going to remove his eye, wash if off, and put it back in.

But for now, Amandu Bangura appeared asleep, not from general anesthesia but from weariness, no doubt aided by the comfort of a bed in the cool operating room. After all, he and his nephew had walked ten kilometers to get to the Kissy Eye Clinic, a Mecca for eye care sorely needed in this African country of Sierra Leone. News of the surgical team's arrival traveled quickly.

His above-average height allowed me to remember seeing Amandu that morning. He joined hundreds of African patients who, like ants racing in and out of their hills in search of food for their queen, streamed in from the city streets and villages, down dusty paths, their thongs and bare feet pushing clouds of red dirt off their heels, focusing their energies on getting to the clinic. The tall white doctor was their hope for sight.

Amandu Bangura was among the first to arrive, long before the sun had risen to meet the day, clutching the arm of his nephew, Foday, a rail-thin youngster, ten—or twelve-years old. It's hard to determine age in Africa when one often doesn't enjoy two meals in one day.

While Foday's ragged Dallas Cowboys T-shirt hung limply off lean shoulders, Amandu's dress code was more formal: a long-sleeved, ankle-length, pale blue cotton tunic, once enhanced, now frayed by darker embroidery at the collarless neck and sleeve hems. On closer inspection, spots that appeared to be the result of a tie-dye project were actually splotchy memories of food and body functions. Perched on his white natural Afro and adding another four inches to his reedy frame, was a tightly coiled turban.

After many hours of quiet waiting, he was directed to the operating table. Now the surgeon's hands rested on his forehead, poised for the first incision. The sterile drape moved in rhythm to his mouth breathing, forcing it to rise and fall around his mouth and nose. The drape was a blessing. His breath, unfiltered, would stop a train. Cleaning his face prior to surgery introduced me to each line etched in his narrow, sunken face, small unseeing eyes hunkered under bushy brows, the white stubble on his upper lip and chin, and the colorless, cracked lips hovering over the only tooth in his head.

I was fascinated by his feet: two nails missing, his soles no stranger to the miles of ground he'd covered during his eighty-two years. The gnarled arthritic knuckles of his hand, which had grasped the head of his walking stick that morning, now rested quietly at his side.

Yes, for now he was at peace, perhaps even dreaming of a new tomorrow.

Living Up to Love

Joan Fedor

"Someone's in there, in the back seat of the car." Bob stood by the door leading to the garage.

When I prodded, he opened the door and pointed. No one was there. Nor had people taken him on a trip "way out" one night, for some unclear purpose. He acted casual but certain they needed him, so said he stayed until they brought him back.

Bob seldom went to bed when I did, but his nights became longer and longer. I would wake to see the light through the bedroom transom. Too many times I found him sleeping upright on a stiff wooden chair. No amount of jostling or cajoling could move him. I would return to bed and lie rigid, attempting to sleep again. I grew to hate that light through the transom.

But the nights could vary. There was no sleep for either of us when, at three a.m., he begged for the car keys to go to Tony's for a haircut. Or the less and less frequent bath nights when the plugged-in electric heater hummed ominously as the water ran. Imploring entrance led to my acceptance that bathing was seldom worth it, a difficult decision for an always fastidious man.

Those who watch their loved one sink into the quicksand of Alzheimer's are plunged willy-nilly into a "new beginning." There is the realization that no one would ever love you as he did. The casual male friend who puts his arm around you for a picture cannot know how much it hurts to realize the loss of intimacy and companionship of a living loved one. Not only that, you become the worst kind of paradox: a husband's mother with all the painful contradictions. Disciplining him or exercising tough love become techniques for your survival rather than his improvement. His behavior would not get better, and he would not grow up to be a better person. As one beleaguered wife complained, "He won't mind." It is much to learn that we cannot be successful.

The "new beginning" of coping remained an ongoing narrative. Medication helped and perplexed. For a month or two he plugged in the telephone correctly and even went to bed regularly. He was ready with packed suitcase for a short trip. The notion that he could do more created insidious decisions: a cruise, the anniversary trip to the Grand Canyon. But the lighted nights began again too close to cancel plans. "They" don't sufficiently warn you that a possible two years of relief can end abruptly at five months. You feel naïve, betrayed, a failure.

Talking about it resulted in blatant ironies. The Alzheimer's plague creates an oral history that defies hierarchy. There are too many stories for yours to prevail. Mentioning my husband inevitably led to listening rather than telling. The "funny" tales won the day. Support groups do give good advice—don't let him drive, buy him a bracelet, take him to day care. They do try. After a while the extensive literature repeats and exploits. It's a scary and intriguing subject.

As time passed, choices needed to be made. Becoming the sole decision maker for the first time ranged from paying bills and doing income taxes to what am I to do about Bob. The days reverberated with tension. Hiding all sink and bath stoppers was the only insurance against flooding. Burned muffins smoked from the microwave. The bathroom stool replaced the wooden chair as the nightly marathon seat. Fried hot dogs became the most acceptable meal. Tables, desks, counters littered with "important material" were closely guarded. A walk ended in a dark rescue by the posse. Too often strife ruled.

Then one day I told him that he needed to move to the care center where he had spent successful respite time and made friends. He did not protest. I saw him to bed in a separate room in our home, and he was in a good mood. The next morning I found him, well dressed, he thought, in a new pair of pajamas and a baseball cap. He believed that he had already moved. He hugged me and said he was happy and surprised to see me there. I drove him with his suitcase to the care center. He asked why I was crying when they came to greet him and said, "Don't cry, honey." It's difficult now to admit that I never liked to be called honey.

*　　*　　*

Now I was to live alone in the house where he put all the furniture together and where we were so excited about being retired and free. This phase of my "new beginning" included watching him decline over fewer than two years to become someone who did not know me but said again, one month before he died, not to cry when he saw tears. It was a fleeting moment, and I have tried to use it as a hallmark for my ongoing "new beginning."

For most of our fifty-one years, Bob and I were a happy and independent couple. We had each other and that mattered most. As I gradually lost him, I realized how much I needed my family and the kindness of friends, as well as strangers. My new life will never measure up to my old one. I am humbled and often afraid. I realize, however, that without the strengths of the old one a new beginning would not be possible. Bob's love was a legacy that I try not to trash with moping.

Education in A Country School
A Fragment

Vivian Wood

I don't actually remember my first day at that one-room country school where I began my formal education, but I certainly know the tale I told when I came home. My parents repeated the story for years, and it always got a polite laugh from relatives and friends. I don't remember the point at which I understood why people were expected to laugh.

According to family lore, in response to a question about how many students there were on the first day, I said to my mother, "Well, all the seats were full but one—and that's where I was sitting."

Not long ago I drove past the site of the school. All that remains is the old well with its rusty pump. For a moment I was tempted to see whether vigorous thrusts of the old pump handle would bring up from subterranean depths the remembered cool delicious water with which we refreshed ourselves after a rambunctious game of sheep pen's down or handy-over.

I remember the teacher trying to staunch the flow of blood from a wound on the back of my head with cold water from the well while my schoolmates huddled around. The wound came from a piece of steel off an old school desk flung by a pursuing schoolmate in one of the many chase games we played. In those days country schoolteachers were nurses, doctors, psychologists, social workers, custodians, and what-have-you. There were no school buses where I lived. The teacher drove out to school from town every school day and picked me up on the way.

She opened the schoolhouse and got things ready for the day before most of the pupils arrived. As a six-year-old, I probably wasn't much help to her, but two eighth-graders aided her. In winter, they carried in coal for the pot-bellied stove that occupied the center of the schoolroom and shoveled snow from the path.

I can remember shivering on cold winter mornings until the teacher got a fire going in the stove. The kindling was corncobs furnished by a neighboring farmer. It was some time before the coal was ignited and gave out real warmth. Sometimes the stove got red-hot and students whose desks were too close had to move elsewhere temporarily. When there was snow, scads of wet mittens and boots were set to dry around the stove.

In some ways my remembrance of recesses—short ones in mid-morning and mid-afternoon and a longer one at noontime—is more vivid than that of class time. I vaguely remember my mother saying that once I learned to read, I wanted to sit around all the time reading. I can imagine what a wonderful new world reading opened to me, but I don't remember letting it interfere with my playtime. Perhaps the teacher, early on, recognized the need to channel my energy and sociability.

But I did learn! There were three girls in first grade. Right at first there were four, but the fourth girl cried continuously, and the teacher recruited the other three every day to take her home. After two or three weeks, she stopped coming. Perhaps her family decided to wait until the next year to start her education. I never knew.

A running feud existed among the remaining three first-graders. It was always two united against the unfortunate third. There seemed to be no rhyme nor reason as to who would be oddman-out. About every third day I was the unlucky one. That meant that when we were called up to the long bench in front of the teacher's desk to recite, I was unmercifully pinched.

The unwritten rules, as I remember them, were that two were united to bedevil the third—all without letting the teacher see them—while the victim was required to keep a straight face and show no signs of distraction. I do believe this little game went on for the full school year. Who knows what character traits it instilled in us!

The school period that I enjoyed the most occurred at the end of the week. On Friday afternoons, pupils from all eight grades competed in learning games invented by the teacher. One of the students, for example, would put the first letter of a lake, a mountain, or a city on the blackboard and indicate with dashes how many letters the name contained. The pupil who guessed the name got to go to the board and try to stump the other students. This person got to stay at the board as long as no one could guess the names of the places to which clues were given.

Geography was a favorite subject. How exotic those names of faraway places must have seemed to those farm children, many of whom had never been much farther than the county seat.

Then there were spelling bees where I soon learned to hold my own. We developed little tricks to remember a spelling. To this day if someone asks me to spell "geography," you're apt to hear me say under my breath, "George Ellen's old grandmother rode a pig home yesterday."

Our teacher must have been talented to create an environment in which students of such diverse ages were able to learn together. For years, as school consolidation proceeded, I believed I must have had a poor education in that little country school—a school named *Enterprise*. After all, how could an instructor do much teaching when she had pupils from eight grade levels? In more recent years, I've come to reassess that observation. Modern educators have learned the value of cross-grading where children of different ages learn together and from each other.

The country school seems to have worked for me. It wasn't until high school that I attended a school in town—and not a very big town at that. Many years later I earned a Ph.D. degree from a world-renowned university in the nation's second largest city. I give some credit to the young woman in that first country school I attended for my overcoming the odds against a poor farmer's daughter going on to college and getting a Ph.D. She gave us a motto at the end of the school year—May 1929—in a little brochure, now yellow with age, a motto which I must have taken to heart: "Live to learn, and you will learn to live."

My First House

Greta Bryan

Oh, yes, of course I remember my first house. I'm six years old, after all. I'd have to say it was really old, at least its tired white paint made it look old . . . had a saggy porch that wrapped around half the house. Max, my dog, slept there and barked at everybody. It was right next door to the preacher's house. My friend Carolyn lived there and, besides having dresses alike, we played a lot of school.

So what can a six-year-old remember, you ask. To be honest, only the good stuff and the bad stuff, I guess. Not the in-between stuff that Joanne Porter wrote in her diary-with-a-key every day. She was a sixth grader and wore a bra.

The good stuff was starting to school. The bad stuff takes more time. For starters, that house did not have a bathroom, so you know what was out back, and you also know—if you remember the climate section in your geography book—that it gets cold in an Iowa winter. But at least the bugs are dead in the winter, not like summer when you take your chances with spiders and bees, who like to hang around outhouses. Is it true that only girl bees sting? Well, it must have been a girl bee that got me on the cheek—and I'm not talking about the one on my face. Do you know how embarrassing it is to fly out of a toilet with your underpants around your ankles?

As long as I'm on the bad stuff, I'll briefly mention that brother Don bribed me with a stick of gum to say "shit" THEN told my mother. She had no tolerance for cuss words, especially since we lived next to the preacher. She washed my mouth out with soap. I bawled and blew soap rings for days. I exaggerate sometimes. Maybe you'd also like to know that I got a scooter when the boys got bikes for Christmas. I mean how far can you ride on a scooter anyway?

Oh, yes, I remember my first house next to the preacher. I remember my bed, no I again exaggerate . . . it was a cot. A cot stationed in the corner of the dining room. Why, you ask? There was only one bedroom and one big, really big closet where the boys' bed hit both walls. The best part of the cot was the window next to it. I could see the day before anybody else got up in the morning.

I could go on and on about the day Mom was taken really fast to the hospital to have her appendix out. Or the day my oldest brother found a jar in the basement . . . a jar full of money, mind you. Never did know who belonged to that jar of money. I sure don't remember getting any of it.

Oh yes, I remember my first house. I *am* six years old, you know.

My Six Minutes of Fame with *Horace Heidt*

Evelyn Shipley

While many of you have the fun of collecting, going to flea markets and large radio meets, and then restoring a lot of those found old radios, I have fun and many memories of doing something completely different—but still connected with radios.

In my youth, I loved to sing, play the piano and later, yes, whistle. I did all the usual things that one who loves to perform does, like church choirs, solos, musical theater groups, home shows, private parties, and more.

I attended the College of Music in Cincinnati, Ohio, and later joined the AGVA, American Guild of Variety Artists. This meant I could get paid and led to spots on shows at local nightclubs in and around Cincinnati. It gave me the confidence to do later what I loved most, singing on the radio. Back in those days, there were many live broadcasts to give talent like myself a chance to perform on the radio. Later came what we called "canned music." This meant the end of an era.

Gene Autry, the cowboy star, owned a station in Phoenix called KPHO. I lived in that city for several years, and I decided to try out for a spot on his station. The program director listened to my audition and asked me if I was willing to go on the air "sustaining."

"Sure," I said, unaware that "sustaining" meant you did not get paid.

He told me that a salesman had to go out and sell me, which fortunately for me he did. This was one of many lessons I learned throughout my career. Later, I was to perform on both KPRC in Houston, Texas, and WKRC in Cincinnati.

Horace Heidt, a well-known bandleader in the bygone era of the 1950s, sent his advance man to a particular region where he planned a performance. The advance man would audition talent at one of the local radio stations. It was widely advertised in the adjoining states, and ultimately he would hear at least four hundred auditions.

Five acts were chosen to perform in Phoenix at the Encanto Bowl, where thousands would come to see Horace Heidt and his Musical Knights perform—along with the five chosen from these auditions. I was one of the lucky five. It was a lot of fun. I can say that Horace Heidt was one lovely man with a most gracious personality.

When I sang in Phoenix, the accordion player, Dick Contino, was on the same program. He, too, was very modest and very talented.

A couple of years later, I moved to Houston. Again, the same advance man for Horace Heidt came to see and listen to the talent of the surrounding area. Again, I thought, why not? So, I went to the studio to sing AND whistle for my audition.

The advance man said when I walked up to the microphone, "Haven't I seen you before?"

I smiled and told him that was true—in Phoenix.

He returned the smile and later I was told I'd been chosen for the second time.

Why do I say, "Six Minutes of Fame with Horace Heidt"? Each act was allowed about three minutes. I had three minutes in Phoenix and three in Houston to do my thing—to sing and to whistle. This totals six minutes, right?

I might add that my mother never wanted me to whistle, especially out in public. Her favorite saying to me was, "Whistling girls and crowing hens always come to some bad end."

So far, so good, Mother.

This article first appeared in the *New Mexico Radio Collectors Club Newsletter*, Fall 2006.

This Ticket to Disneyland

Judy Neigoff

I am not a keeper. The miscellaneous detritus of life that comes my way either gets filed in its appropriate place or unceremoniously thrown away. So why do I keep this Disneyland ticket stub that is propped up against the stained glass lamp on my desk?

The ticket came out of my New Directions fanny pack when I came back from this year's annual Christmas "Holiday Happiness" tour where we take develop-mentally disabled adults to Disneyland for Christmas. Maybe the memory of the joy on my traveler's face when I wheeled him in his wheelchair down Disneyland's bustling Main Street and through Snow White's Castle made me pause before throwing it away.

Mickey Mouse in his red Sorcerer's robe is printed on this ticket. I remember when my parents took me to see that movie when I was a child. I laughed at Mickey's foolery, swelled with the crescendos in the classical music, and hid my eyes behind my hands during the scary part when the broomsticks came alive.

My hand reaches out to toss this ticket, but I hesitate. The Mickey Mouse Club TV show was my mainstay as a child. The only way my mother could get me to practice the piano was to suggest that if I got good enough, I could be a guest performer on the show. If she forgot to call me in from play at five p.m. to watch, my whole evening was devastated. I knew every Mouseketeer by name and sang the theme song often enough to drive my brother and sister crazy.

I should put this ticket with my first Disneyland ticket! Disneyland opened in 1955. I begged and pleaded with my parents for two whole years before they broke down and got me there. My father had a business trip to Los Angeles, and he arranged to take me—only me, not my mother, brother or sister, only me—along with him so I could go to Disneyland.

We flew on a jet plane together from our home in New York to California. He hired a college student to take care of me while he tended to business, but I took care of the college student because I knew everything and everywhere to go in Disneyland. I must have run her ragged. I had a Brownie box camera and took pictures. Now I search for that scrapbook and, yes, here is my first Disneyland ticket and many carefully pasted black-and-white photos.

Now I know why I kept this ticket. Because it now has a place in my Disneyland scrapbook. After all, Disneyland is for children of all ages.

The First House I Ever Owned

Vivian Wood

I bought my first house when I was 65. I had toyed with the idea of home ownership earlier in my life but never got serious about it. An apartment with far fewer maintenance worries fit my busy life style of teaching and research at the University of Wisconsin.

But when I retired at 65, I made a radical change in my life. During my Marine Corps days in World War II, I had been stationed in Southern California. The aura of the West grabbed me then, and retirement provided the opportunity to return to the West.

At the University of Wisconsin, I had been involved during the mid-1960s analyzing data from a study about retirement and migration, carried out by colleagues in another department. Hearing about my expertise in gerontology, they recruited me to look at differences among male retirees who stayed in their home communities, those who moved to regular communities in a warm climate, and those who moved to age-segregated communities—Sun City, Arizona, being one of those in which data had been collected from its retiree residents.

I was intrigued that the retirees in Sun City seemed to be more active, involved, "with it" than retirees who stayed in place. The explanation may be that retirees who migrated to age-segregated communities were generally healthier, more educated, and had higher incomes. Nevertheless, Sun City residents were more unconventional—willing to try new things.

In 1985, a couple of years before my planned retirement at 65, I ran across an ad about visiting Sun City West, a follow-up of the original Sun City in Arizona. I decided to go investigate. A couple of friends thought it was a good idea and joined me. We planned our outing for the two-week spring break.

A colleague, who was a visiting professor at ASU-Tempe that semester, was going skiing over the break and offered us a week's use of her rented condo in Scottsdale. Arizona's sunshine sounded good after a Wisconsin winter. Following a week of exploring Scottsdale and environs, we headed west on Bell Road.

The drive to Sun City West along the mostly two-lane road was interesting in itself. Some horse farms, lots of orange groves, some businesses and stretches of empty lots. Our excitement mounted as we reached Sun City West and turned up R. H. Johnson Boulevard. We located the Visitors Center and were directed to the apartment that was to be our home for almost a week.

Sun City was founded in 1960. It was "built out" by 1985, and homes were being sold in Sun City West. We joined hundreds of others on the tour wagons that took us all around Sun City West. We ended up at the Del Webb Model Homes, which were said to be the largest tourist attraction in Arizona. Del Webb kept track of which states tourists came from. Illinois and California were tops, as I recall.

We were given a free breakfast and free tickets to the Sundome—treated royally all around. We explored Sun City West, returned to the Sundome a few times, but kept going back to the Model Homes. The homes were furnished, and it was easy to imagine living in one, picking oranges from a tree in the back and having breakfast on the patio. We kept reminding ourselves that we came to look, not to make decisions.

A week after we returned to work in Wisconsin, we compared notes and sheepishly confessed that we were really "taken" with Sun City West and had begun to think of it as a place to retire.

Del Webb's staff—like the good salesmen they were—kept in touch with me and sent me much literature. I studied the models, pored over and over my finances, and gradually made definite plans to retire. I would go to Sun City West on my holiday break at the end of 1986. My two younger friends who had accompanied me before were sure I would need them to help make decisions.

We stayed in the Vacation Homes as before and went to the sales department at the Model Homes. I was shown the suggested lot on which my home was to be constructed. It was on Yosemite Drive, which was plotted out on a map but didn't really exist yet. R.H. Johnson Boulevard went only as far as the Library. From Meeker Drive (which did exist) one could see acres and acres of brown earth with stakes and string. It was difficult to imagine the community it would become.

I had already decided which model I wanted. Many additional decisions had to be made about carpeting, light fixtures, cupboards, tiling, colors, upgrades. A middle-aged woman was assigned to help me. Of course, my friends were sure their inputs were needed. By this time, Christmas Eve was approaching. Our helper, it soon became apparent, was anxious to get away on a trip to see her grandchildren. She tried to hurry me along without appearing to do so. When I made a decision, my friends would caution, "Have you considered this?" We were making slow progress.

My friends remembered an errand they had to do and left—to the great relief of my helper. "We can wrap this up quickly," she said. But back came my friends after deciding they shouldn't abandon me when so many important decisions were still needed. We labored on.

Eventually all decisions were made, my helper went off to see her grandchildren, and my friends and I went to Sedona to spend a celebratory three days in a fancy resort. My final five months of work, a wonderful retirement party, many tearful goodbyes, and promises of visits lay ahead.

Den of Antiquity—Old Radios

Evelyn Shipley

Jan and Dan had a wonderful marriage of more than twenty-five years. Many people would ask what their secret was to such a happy union. Each would come up with the same thoughts, such as caring, sharing, respect, humor, and some shared interests.

Jan knew that in a few weeks Dan would have another birthday, but what could she find that would please him this year? She gave it quite a bit of thought, and while reading the newspaper—the want ads—Jan thought she found her answer. Someone was selling their entire collection of old radios. Great! Perhaps she would find a real treasure for her husband. A phone call and appointment set Jan off to see the man's collection of old radios.

"You'll be sorry." Jan remembers those haunting words the avid radio collector said to her. He was about to part with a prized old radio from his huge collection.

Jan was optimistic that she'd found the perfect gift for her husband, a bit of nostalgia. She was curious, why would she be sorry? She was not sure she wanted to know the answer.

If she introduced her husband to the fascinating world of old radios, the collector warned, his newfound interest would leave little time for anything or anyone else, including her.

Was he speaking from experience, she wondered?

He was.

"This love affair of mine with old radios is what caused wives #1 and #2 to fly the coop," he readily admitted. "I really thought I was keeping each of them happy. When each had sleeping problems, I immediately had the answer, or so I thought. I just suggested that they think of an old radio, and they would soon fall asleep. Somehow it did not work for them. Too bad," he said, "it works for me every time."

As he continued, it soon became apparent that wife #3 was about to take the same path as the preceding two. "She thinks I am an obsessed radio collector. The ultimatum: get rid of the radios or start looking for wife #4. A tough decision."

A tough decision indeed! Whether he would regret his decision remained to be seen. He opted for his wife.

Now what should Jan do? Continue as planned and purchase one of these remnants of the past—something that she thought would really please her husband—or after hearing this man's story forget the whole idea? "Onward and upward" had always been her motto. Why change now?

Jan knew nothing about old radios at this point only that there was a difference between battery-operated and radios powered by electricity. When the seller showed her "breadboards" she could only think that they did not look complete for they were not in a cabinet of any kind. She did not think that they could be worth very much. Later she found out how wrong she was not only in value but what they actually were, which was a set of radio parts assembled on a board. This came to be known as a breadboard radio.

Dan had spoken of his fascination for early radios as a child in Nebraska. That's it! Jan thought.

Her acquisition was a rather rusty metal chassis with an emblem that proudly displayed "Atwater Kent." It had only one tube.

Dan's birthday arrived, and Jan proudly presented her husband with what she knew was surely a treasure.

When Dan first looked at it, his expression did not match her expectations.

"I hope that you didn't pay very much for this," he said.

Jan asked, "Was fifty dollars too much?"

"Yes," he replied.

She knew he did not mean to be unkind, but he informed her that it was really "just a bit of junk."

*　　*　　*

Now, many years later Jan looks back and says that this was the best fifty dollars she ever spent.

That Atwater Kent model 35 radio was completely restored by her husband, and set him on a goal to purchase other old radios, magazines, earphones, test equipment. Dan became interested especially in the technical evolution of radios. He enjoys restoring each acquired radio to its original state. Dan has enjoyed many happy days and moments and shared thoughts with other radio collectors.

Jan and Dan are still married and their hopes are that the seller is too. Long may they sleep well. Jan and Dan say they do and that Dan does not have to tell Jan any bedtime stories either.

Jan has been educated regarding her husband's new hobby. She now knows such names as Grebe, Federal, Atwater Kent, and Crosley. She knows the distinction between RCA Aeriola and Radiola. She understands about many other battery-operated radios, and, yes, especially about Atwater Kent "breadboards." The earlier models are not housed in cabinets but the later ones are.

Jan watches her husband derive many, many hours of pleasure from this hobby. Just to see his face when he unpacks an antique radio is like watching a kid at Christmastime, pure joy!

Looking back on that time when Jan bought the "piece of junk" can you hear her complaining? No way. Good things come from surprise beginnings.

My First House

Judy Neigoff

17 Poplar Street, Elmsford, NY. LY2-6878. That address and telephone number are still emblazoned on my memory despite learning them almost sixty years ago. My parents made me memorize these as a small child "in case I got lost." But I had no intention of getting lost, as I loved my house.

My first house was a stucco, two-story, boxy affair, white with dark brown trim. It had a porch off the kitchen door that was framed by low walls, perfect for coming and going and sitting with friends. It had a formal front door on the other side that no one used. The garage was not attached and sat at the end of the driveway that snaked up the side of the house. Big trees and lots of lawn surrounded everything.

My bedroom on the second floor was my special place. It was originally just a closet off the master bedroom, but after three kids, my parents did a little rearranging of walls and doors upstairs so that we would each have our own room. They thought that I got shortchanged with the smallest room, but I loved that it was long and skinny and compact. I even had a window overlooking Poplar Street.

The rest of the house was probably typical 1950s suburban. I remember the speckled linoleum tiles in our playroom, the hush of our formal living room with its blue carpet and grand piano, and climbing on and off the built-in wooden benches in the breakfast nook. Our basement, however, was the future. My father's workbench lined the far wall, covered with wondrous tools and blinking electronic instruments. There I spent hours working with my father, repairing TV sets and toasters.

It was a good, solid house—and I spent a good, solid childhood there.

An Imaginary Box

Elaine Sievers

I do not keep—and never have kept—a box of cherished articles. I am sorry about this. It would be most pleasant to touch and hold special articles and to enjoy the memories each would bring. I do have happy memories that I want to keep, happy memories that I don't want to slip away. So, because I do not have a real box, I shall design my own imaginary box, and then I shall fill it with memories that are special and dear to me.

This imaginary memory box is going to be a private box. Selfishly, I don't want to share it or the memories that fill it with my family or with my friends. I want to, alone, take out each memory and cherish it in my own way. By myself, I want to quietly enjoy dwelling in the nostalgia of the past.

The box will be beautiful, tastefully fine and elegant, covered in a soft fabric of periwinkle blue. The inside lining will be luxurious, creamy satin, and the lid will be secured with a deep blue satin ribbon tied in a perfect bow. Because my memories will be nurtured and cherished, they deserve to be housed in a worthy and estimable setting.

*　　*　　*

In the box will be memories of my childhood and of my mother and my father and my sister and my brothers. My family is gone now. So I will sort out the happy times of my childhood from the sad times and put only the happy times in my box. I know that I will cry softly as these family memories are gently placed in the box and, later, I will shed tears as I take them out to ponder upon.

I will carefully put into the box, too, memories of my children. When these memories are taken out of the box, they will bring smiles. I want to never forget the growing up years of my children and the moments of joy that my children brought to me.

I want to remember the good years of my marriage, so I will pack into my imaginary memory box some very special times in my relationship with my husband. When these memories are taken out of the box, I will feel a sense of safety and assurance.

There will be memories of friends in my imaginary box. Friends' memories will be pleasant, and I will feel grateful for each as I take it out to reminisce.

The memory of Kitty will be tucked into the bottom of the box. There, my wonderful Siamese "Kitty" will nestle in the soft, satin folds. Her beautiful blue eyes will look up to slyly assure me that she will keep our secret that we were always and forever pledged to be best friends.

Each stage of my life will have a special place of honor in my box. I want to remember how it felt to be a child, a young adult, a student, a career person, a married woman, a mother, and an older woman. Again, I will insist on putting into the box only the happiest memories of each stage, so that I may rejoice in reliving them.

*   *   *

These special memories will wait patiently for the keeper of the box to untie the blue satin bow and lift the lid in eager anticipation of spending a deeply satisfying time remembering and reminiscing.

When, one day, I decide to open the box, the happy memories will spill out with abandon—as if waiting for the occasion. They will gently float outward and upward, blending together, and then they will waft into every inch of my private space. I will surely be enveloped in a warm glow of joy.

Isn't that what memories are for?

My Best Christmas Present

Evelyn Shipley

I have received many wonderful Christmas presents throughout my lifetime, but one stands out as my very best, the one that made me the happiest.

As a young girl I, like so many others, wrote letters during World War II to a lot of my friends and to some relatives who were in various branches of service. This included my brother, **Howard Baur**, who was in the Navy and saw fighting in the South Pacific. Other friends are:

Mel Skiff, a pilot in the 8th Air Force, who flew B24 aircraft over the Ploesti oilfields in Europe.

Bob and **Frank Hosea**, brothers both in the Infantry who fought in the Battle of the Bulge in Europe.

Harvey Morgan, a coxswain in the Coast Guard piloting landing craft in places such as Guadalcanal and Iwo Jima. He sent me a postcard showing a landing craft with someone in back steering the boat with his head down. He said that is what he did and, yes, with his head down.

Chester Baker, a tail gunner on a B-24, flying missions over Europe. Had his plane been hit and everyone else bailed out, his chances would have been slim for making it out as he would have had to crawl through a tunnel from back to front to escape while the plane spiraled downward.

As an aside, some years ago when I lived in Albuquerque, New Mexico, a B-24 was brought to the city and anyone who wished to could go out to the airport and see this aircraft. I went alone as my husband was at work. I was able to climb up through the bomb bay to get inside the plane and could see where the pilot, co-pilot, and navigator sat, where the gunners sat in the middle of the airplane, and, yes, where the tail gunner sat. I came away with a better appreciation for what some of these fellows went through.

Allen Ziegler, in the Signal Corps in England.

Harry Derrick, in the Navy.

Bill Thoney, in the Seabees in the South Pacific.

My cousin **Ernie Gesenhues, a** medic in the South Pacific. He saw some of the worst fighting in those islands. When he was inducted into the Army he had coal black hair but when he returned home he was completely gray.

Marold Baker, a sharpshooter and an instructor at Camp Shelby, Mississippi, during the entire war. He was good with people and knew a lot about guns, so I can see that he would have been an asset to the Army in this capacity.

*   *   *

When World War II ended in 1945, one by one ALL of these men came home safely and none had serious wounds. I was so grateful, and that Christmas was the very best to give thanks for so many blessings. All my friends and relatives from the various services were back in the United States with their families, safe and sound.

My Family's Hanukkah

Judy Neigoff

By the window you can see the glow
From my Menorah on newly fallen snow . . .

My family's Hanukkah was a quiet, intimate affair. While in the outside world people were singing overly cheerful Christmas carols, decorating gaudy trees, and frantically buying presents, we were celebrating a different holiday a different way. My parents made clear to us children that Hanukkah was not the "Jewish Christmas." Hanukkah is actually a minor holiday, a celebration of the Jewish people uniting under Judah Maccabee in the year 164 BCE to drive out the occupying Assyrian-Greek forces and rededicate the Temple in Jerusalem to Judaism.

On the first night of Hanukkah, my mother would get out our Menorah. It was shiny brass and stood a good foot-and-a-half high. She would set it down in the middle of the dinner table. The eight arms looked bare and empty, awaiting the candles. Then, when we were all seated and quiet and ready for dinner, my father would ceremoniously open the colorful Hanukkah candle box and carefully extract two candles. One he fitted in the center, taller arm of the Menorah. This was the Shamus, the candle that lights all the others. The single candle for the first night was fitted in the first of the eight arms. We would each hold our breath as my mother struck a match and lit the Shamus. Then, slowly, she removed the Shamus and brought it to the first candle, lighting it as we all said the blessing together:

Blessed art Thou, Lord our God, King of the universe, who sanctified us by Your commandments and commanded us to kindle the lights of Hanukkah.

The Shamus was returned to its place in the Menorah and we all stared, mesmerized by the flickering candlelight, thinking, perhaps, about how this lighting of the Menorah symbolized the miracle of the Eternal Light in the ancient Temple in Jerusalem, rekindling and burning for eight days until new oil could be made. But the spell was too soon broken when my parents pulled out a small Hanukkah present for each of us.

No Jewish holiday is complete without traditional foods. On Hanukkah we eat foods fried in oil to commemorate that miracle of the Eternal Light. The sizzle of frying potato latkes and the smell of oil and applesauce make this dinner a Hanukkah dinner. And we can always count on chocolate Hanukkah gelt for dessert. Sometimes we play dreidel, a noisy gambling game with a four-sided wooden top. That is where the gelt comes in—our piles of chocolate growing or diminishing with the luck of the spin.

And the best thing about Hanukkah is that we do it all over again the next night, and the next, for eight nights, watching the Menorah's eight arms fill day by day. I always loved the last night best, when the Menorah was fully aglow and my Mother would put it in the window to shine out on the newly fallen snow.

LIFE SKETCHES

Babcha

Ann Winsor

Her blue eyes twinkle as she beckons me closer. She is reading my lips for she is totally deaf.

The rest of the family have little to do with her because of her inability to understand their speech—and she speaks only in Polish, her native language. She happily recounts tales of her life, her experiences in raising her children—two daughters and a son (who went on to Harvard University and eventually taught in the Harvard Dental School). Peter, her husband, was an alcoholic and not much help.

Babcha, meaning Grandmother, is turning men's frayed shirt collars and using her Singer sewing machine to restitch them, adding to the family income. I am sitting close to her so that I can catch each word she says in Polish. I am delighted to have her spend so much time with me, and also I know that soon she will say, "Let's go into the kitchen and have a bite to eat. I have some good bread, and I'll make us coffee."

She bustles about, and I sit patiently watching her. Occasionally, she will turn around and wink at me. "Look at my kitchen floor. It is so clean, you could eat off of it!" And she is right. In fact, her entire, modest tenement was so tidy that I loved just looking at each braided rug and the polished pieces of furniture placed here and there.

As we eat our simple fare of bread and coffee, she smiles at me. I feel welcomed and loved by this gracious old lady, my mother's sister.

A Visit from Great-Aunt Emma

Vivian Wood

After more than half a century, I still remember Great-Aunt Emma in all her immensity. As long as I live, when I hear the name "Emma" I shall think of a great huge woman. Aunt Emma was physically huge, it's true, but it was more than that. She had what I recognize now as a zest for life—a zest exceeded only by her zest for food. She could eat more than anyone I ever knew—and I was used to seeing farm hands wolf down plates of the food my mother cooked on the old kitchen range. We children used to bet—in secret, of course—how many pieces of chicken Great-Aunt Emma could eat at one sitting.

At the noontime meal she would polish off three plates of fried chicken and a dozen ears of corn. Afterwards the adults would sit around the decimated table, lethargic in the hot afternoon air. We children sat in the background and listened to the grown-ups talk. Actually I don't know how much we listened. Mostly we watched.

Great-Aunt Emma with her hearty laugh that shook her ample bosom, her gold-rimmed glasses and gold-filled teeth that flashed as she talked, was a strong presence—at least in my memories of an Ohio farm in the 1930s. Those were pretty dreary times on the farms of America, and a visit from Aunt Emma stood out like a red bandana on a vast gray landscape.

In my memory my aunt arrives at the farm alone in a touring car—big and black with the isinglass side curtains open to let in whatever breezes there were on a hot August day. But I remember her in the passenger seat—an expansive woman sitting back and viewing the world majestically. Someone had to have driven her down from Toledo—a place I had no conception of except that it was far away. Years later I was surprised to learn I could drive the distance in an hour and a half.

When I try hard to conjure up a picture in my memory of Aunt Emma's arrival, I remember vaguely Uncle Frank—probably a normal-sized man but he paled in size beside his wife—quiet, gray and retiring. He seemed as colorless as she was colorful. I hope Uncle Frank wouldn't mind my forgetting him so easily any more than he seemed to mind Great-Aunt Emma always being in the limelight. He seemed to enjoy basking in the warmth of her shadow, just as did all of us.

In retrospect, I think Aunt Emma and Uncle Frank must have stayed with Grandpa and Grandma, who lived in town. There must have been some consideration of their staying with us on the farm as I remember Mama being concerned about whether the bed slats on the old farm bedstead would hold. We kids talked excitedly about the bed falling down in the middle of the night with a terrible crash and were a little disappointed when Aunt Emma didn't stay overnight with us. As far as I know my Grandma's bed always held up under her bulk.

Aunt Emma was always a big tease. "What caused those two bumps on your chest?" she'd ask me. "I bet a bee stung you!" I was embarrassed to death over those references to my budding adolescence but, despite the mortification, I had a warm feeling about her teasing. She'd pat my behind and say, "It's okay, Peanuts, you're just growing up." When she used that special nickname no one else ever used, I somehow knew teasing was just her way of being nice.

She was a good sport, too. In the Sunday afternoon ballgame in the pasture south of the barn, she usually took a turn at bat. She could hit a mean ball but refused to run the bases. My kid brother Bugs ran for her. They were quite a team. She'd slam the ball out in left field and Bugs would take off.

Aunt Emma's favorite sport, I'm sure, was eating but playing cards was a close second. Pinochle was her game. The adults stayed up late at night playing cards when she came to visit. We children could hear them laughing and talking after we'd been reluctantly ushered off to bed. "Why can't we stay up and play?"

"Off to bed with you and we'll play tomorrow," Aunt Emma promised. True to her word we got our first lesson in pinochle next day. No "Old Maid" for her! She only believed in "real cards."

Great-Aunt Emma's visit always coincided with the Bates Family Reunion. Most families must have had family reunions in those days. Anyway the park where our family gathered was filled with families, each of which staked out several long wooden tables, which were covered with an odd assortment of tablecloths. Every family picnic basket or box must have contained one special for the occasion. Every mother brought her family's favorite dishes and the tables were soon filled to overflowing. There was always much more than anyone could eat—but we sure tried! Aunt Emma was in her glory!

All the relatives tried to find nice things to say to the mothers about each of their children. "What a pretty little girl!" "What a smart little boy!" For me, it was always, "What a healthy little girl!" I'm afraid I wasn't very appreciative of my health. In fact, I sometimes hated being healthy. But the family reunion was no time to think about that. So many strange cousins to play with! So many new things to do!

I remember once getting into the wrong family reunion. I never noticed the difference—the same big tables groaning with food, grown-ups talking loud and fast over the hubbub to get in all the visiting they could until next year, and kids running around wildly. Before I got to the homemade ice cream, Mama, embarrassed and apologetic, came to claim me and drag me from the bosom of my "new family" whose name I never knew.

Usually Aunt Emma and Uncle Frank left for home after the family reunion. Uncle Frank bore her off in the big touring car with everyone waving wildly and calling to them to "Come back soon" and "See you next year!" We too were bundled into our old Model A Ford and we headed for home. We kids were soon asleep in the back seat with my sister in the front seat with Mama.

It wasn't until the next day that we missed Aunt Emma. Life seemed drab and flat again. Time stretched ahead endlessly with nothing to look forward to. A visit from Aunt Emma next year was too far off to fathom.

Just when things seemed bleakest, Dad told us that if we'd work hard and do our chores, he'd take us to see the animals unloaded when the circus would come to town next week. What fun to get up 'way before sunrise and drive into town in the cool morning air. I had been before! All week I'd tell my younger brothers how the circus people unload the animals from the train. The elephants with their trunks could pick you up and crush you. If a tiger got loose . . . I'd shiver with mock fear and embroider the stories for my brothers' benefit. Great-Aunt Emma was forgotten—'til next year.

One Year with a Very Special Child

Elaine Sievers

You meet the little boy for the first time and you like him. There is something about this child that strikes a warm note in your heart. Perhaps it is his set chin or the straight line of his lips or perhaps it is because he holds his head high over a small, fragile body. With his body language, he is telling you and the world that he is a tough little kid. You know better. You look beneath the façade and you see a frightened child. But you detect a glimmer of courage there, too, and you like that glimmer of courage.

The child was sent to you because he is a 'problem child' and you are known as a skilled 'problem child' teacher. You work, in small groups, with children who are in trouble at school, planning individual programs and making interventions that might make a difference for educational success. The little boy with the set chin and the glimmer of courage is your newest challenge.

You have been told that this boy is underhandedly naughty and that he doesn't measure up academically. He exasperates his teachers because he often chooses not to talk. They think he doesn't talk because, by not communicating, he can be in control. They are probably correct in this assessment.

You observe and watch for signs and clues that will give you some ideas for structuring his learning plan. The boy is small and walks slowly and deliberately and he doesn't smile. He hangs back and watches and waits but you suspect that, as he is watching and waiting, he is taking in and processing much information. You wonder if, perhaps, this is a very smart, clever boy. You guess that he will not cry. He is too proud to cry. While he is sizing up his new teacher and classmates, you can't miss the reticence as you see him quickly choose to be a non-participant. A question addressed to the class is absorbed because there is a slight response in the eyes. But a question personally addressed to him is answered with silence, a silence that you suspect could go on for a long time.

While quietly observing, you talk to yourself, directing your thoughts to him. "I'm your new friend," you say. "You don't know it now, but I'm going to be a very good and caring friend. You will be amazed by what my caring will do for you."

The child senses he is being watched. You give him a sudden radiant smile and he is surprised. *Shall I smile back*, he wonders, *or shall I pretend I didn't notice?* He chooses not to notice but his eyes betray him.

You are a dear, you think, *and very special.* Then you silently give yourself a warning. *Be careful. He is hurting and vulnerable. If you make missteps in your teaching or in your relationship with him, no matter how dear and special he is, this sensitive boy will not be forgiving.*

You work out a plan of action and set your goals. You will ignore that he often will not talk; simply not notice when he doesn't respond. In fact, in the plan you are devising, you will do much ignoring, only noticing when he is doing what you would like him to do. When that happens, you will lavish him with praise. "What wonderful work you do," you will say. Or, "I love how you didn't give up on that problem." You will approach academics in a controlled, methodical way, making sure that there is only success in the first crucial weeks. You decide that, initially, you will try to live through the naughtiness, ignoring what you can. In a flash of inspiration, you decide to place his desk between the desks of two gregarious chatterboxes and then you vow to ignore what you know will be his discomfort with their forced conversations.

For yourself, you review your own lessons in patience. Change will take time so you steel yourself for consistency and tenacity in carrying out your plan.

It turns out to be a trying year for the boy. He has many new lessons to learn and there is resistance. Early progress is slow. It turns out to be a trying year for you, too. More than once you find yourself going back to review your patience lessons but you stick to your plan and remind yourself that this is a very special child you are working with. Indeed, your first wondering 'perhaps' question has turned out to be true. The child is intelligent beyond his years.

After the slow start, the pace of progress picks up. Because of innate intelligence and well-structured lessons, and because of newly found confidence, academic skills improve. Positive strokes prove to be helpful.

One day when you are truly pleased with his work and proudly rave, "Your ability just really astounds me!" he gazes at you calmly and flatly announces, "I can do anything!"

Well, yes, you think to yourself as you are taken aback by his confident declaration. *I do believe you can.*

After a while the boy is more accepting of classroom expectations and the naughtiness slackens off. Some reticence continues but, with the talkative classmates doing their job, he finds it hard to be a total non-communicator. The boy learns that doing good work is satisfying. Very slowly he comes around to the idea that friends share and that friends support each other and that he, too, needs to be a sharing and supporting friend. As his comfort level builds, he finds it easier to smile and sometimes he even laughs. During a class lesson one day you smile to yourself when he bursts out laughing with spontaneous abandon.

The year draws to an end. You are pleased and proud because the child has come a long way. He needed you and you have been able to give him help and support. But he has been a giver, too, although unknowingly, because he has challenged you to care and to work hard and to stay with the program and, ultimately, to make a positive difference in his education.

On the last day of school, when the other children are bouncing around filled with giddy plans for summer fun, the little boy is subdued. As he sits at his desk for the last time he quietly looks at his teacher with tears in his eyes. He doesn't know how to say that he is grateful, and he doesn't know how to say goodbye. Instinctively, you open your arms. Blinking back the tears because brave little boys do not cry, he suddenly comes forward with arms outstretched for the final farewell.

Just as it was on the first day when you met him, you still like this tough little boy. Only this time, on his last day with you, you love this tough little boy. For one entire year he challenged you in every way possible but, while the challenge was being played out and while you were busy watching and monitoring and sticking to your plan, the dear and special 'problem child' slowly but surely staked a claim in your heart. Your tears come, too, and you cry together. You share a pride and gratefulness that only the two of you can understand.

It could be said that, for both of you, for the courageous little boy and for his tenacious teacher, it was one terrific year. For you, you are sure that your time together will always be a positive memory.

Bea

Vivian Wood

It is hard to believe that it's been over twenty years since my friend died. I met Bea when I became a new homeowner in Sun City West. We were in a line to pick up something needed for new residents. We became acquainted as we moved up in the line.

By the time we were ready to move on to the next line-up, we were aware that neither of us knew anyone in Sun City West. As we moved across the big parking lot in front of the Sundome, Bea stumbled and I caught her. Although it seemed unimportant at the time, it was probably an early symptom of the cruel disease that would destroy Bea's life bit by bit.

I left a couple of weeks later to spend the summer with friends in Minnesota. By that time we were friends, and Bea offered to check on the builders who were making an addition to my new home. We talked on the phone several times during the summer.

When I returned in September, my longtime high-school friend Mary was with me to help transport my two cats by car from Wisconsin to Arizona. Bea was glad to see us, and she and Mary hit it off immediately. My cat Missy was aloof but Amos took to Bea. He had a way of insinuating himself into your lap, and Bea loved it. Mary, Bea, and I had a great time for the six weeks Mary stayed.

Of all the friends I've made over the years, Bea was one of the best, also one of the briefest. She was like a flash of lightning on the horizon, bright and shining, then gone.

She was special in many ways. Most important was her sense of humor. She loved a good joke better than anyone I ever knew. I can still hear that contagious laugh and see the way she threw her head back, laughing heartily.

Bea loved to talk, and she was a good conversationalist. At a restaurant or wherever, she engaged surrounding people in conversation, exchanging jokes, ideas about interesting places to see, places to eat, and so on. She had traveled a lot. I remember Afghanistan was her favorite country.

She loved life. I suspect she always did, but perhaps her increasing awareness that her life would be foreshortened made her love it more.

Bea died of Lou Gehrig's disease a year later after losing her ability to speak.

My Favorite Teacher

Greta Manville

Way back in the dark days of BT (Before Television—and a lot of other things), I had an abiding fear of our grade school principal, Ethel Ustick.

When I was in second grade, Miss Ustick had called me into her office and threatened to paddle me for watching, mind you *watching*, a fight that had taken place between a couple of kids who were wrestling on the boulevard grass a block from the school. Indeed, it was a vicious struggle, and I pretended to be Rollo in the *Katzenjammer Kids* cartoon series, hiding behind a big tree and giggling. Miss Ustick, a plump, red-haired old maid who lived with her brother and sister and dressed in styles created by the Victorians, didn't care that I hadn't been an active participant. I'd *been there*, and her remonstrance terrified me, because teachers in those days had big, wooden paddles. The fifth grade teacher even had one with holes in it so the whacks would sting more!

I survived third grade with nothing more physical than weekly checks for mites in our hair and ears (I didn't have any). When it came time to advance to fourth grade, however, I was terrified. I pretended that I was afraid to continue going to that old brick building my father had attended before time began (and Miss Ustick was *his* teacher then), because the concrete trim around the rooftop was crumbling, and I was sure I'd be killed. I pleaded with my mother to send me to another grade school. She tried but couldn't get me in because our small town of five thousand was divided into three rigid school districts, so I was stuck.

Summoning up the mighty courage of a nine-year-old, I ventured into the fourth grade—and soon became enchanted with Miss Ustick and her love for teaching. After we said the Pledge of Allegiance to the flag each morning, she would roll down a huge map of the world for lessons in geography. It was during World War II, so Miss Ustick gave us daily briefings on the troop activities in Europe and the Pacific, straight out of the *Omaha World-Herald*. Throughout the day, she taught us grammar and arithmetic painlessly, and I loved the spelling bees. In those days, Bible study was permitted in schools, so we had daily lessons from the King James version, which served up a great deal of ancient history, though the moral lessons she intended generally escaped her class of little heathens. That same year, Miss Ustick became my Sunday School teacher, and I was so enamored of her vast knowledge (and being a good little suck up) that she let me sit beside her in the fourth row of pews for the Sunday church services, down there where only one or two other brave (or deaf) souls ventured to sit.

I never did get a paddling from Miss Ustick (home was a different matter), nor did I experience the sting of the fifth-grade paddle, though I did learn to appreciate discipline early in life. I also got over calling Ethel "Miss Use-Stick." But was there ever a better name for a school principal?

Caloma, Not an Ordinary Cat

Vivian Wood

Caloma was my all-time favorite cat. I grew up on a farm and knew a long succession of farm cats. But Caloma was a city cat.

She was born in a lab at the University of Chicago where research on cats' brains was conducted. Caloma's mother had given her life for science. The lab assistant, a Ph.D. student studying for his prelims, figured that C-a-l-o-m-a was a combination of letters that helped him remember something about the brain which might be asked on the exam.

The lab assistant and his wife had adopted Caloma, unaware of the taboo against pets at their apartment house. They asked my housemate and me to take care of Caloma while they went on vacation. They never came back to claim her. We didn't mind as we'd become fond of her. We liked to tell friends of her many antics.

One of her favorite tricks was to go out the window and walk along the ledge to a neighbor's window down the way. We cringed to think she might be sampling food set out for lunch or for an after-church meal. But we never heard any complaints.

Caloma always came running when the phone rang as though she were expecting a call. We would ask a friend to give us a ring if we wanted to recall her from one of her treks along the outside ledge. It usually worked.

One day when both my housemate and I were gone, the janitor came to fix a radiator on the sun porch. To get to it, he had to pass through a darkened room. Caloma leaped out and grabbed him around an ankle—a playful trick of hers. The janitor said he thought he would have a heart attack.

After some time, we realized to our dismay that Caloma was pregnant. In due course, she had four female kittens. Being budding feminists, we named them after famous women: Cleopatra, Josephine, Nerfertiti, and Amelia.

The kittens got cuter by the day—and more mischievous. I vividly remember one night when company had taken over the bedroom, and I was sleeping on the foldout couch in the living room. Those kittens spent the night running over the couch, and me, then under the couch and over the couch in a continuous cycle. They were having a great time!

It was the night we realized that living in a small apartment with five cats just wouldn't work. The decision about which cat to keep and which to have the Humane Society pick up was left to me—a heartrending decision!

I chose to keep Caloma, thinking that people looking for a pet were more likely to adopt a cute young kitten than a mature cat. My housemate never forgave me for leaving her home alone when the Humane Society came to pick up the kittens.

After this experience, we had Caloma neutered without delay. All went well until she developed an infection. Her medication didn't seem to help. She grew worse and worse. Fortunately, the veterinarian took on saving her as a personal mission. It took a long time but Caloma did survive. The vet must have taken pity on us and our student budgets. Otherwise, we'd have ended up in the poorhouse.

In the latter stages of Caloma's recovery, the vet gave her hormones, which made her very "sexy," and she escaped from the apartment. Late into the night we went up and down the nearby alleys ringing a bell. Like a phone's ring, the sound of the bell usually brought Caloma running. But not that night.

We went to bed devastated, sure that, despite all we'd been through, we'd lost our cat. Sadly, I went off to work the next morning. Midmorning, I had a call from my housemate. Caloma was back!

My housemate looked out the window and saw Caloma with a motley crew of disreputable-looking males. She rushed out and rescued our cat, who was reluctant to end her adventures. Needless to say, we immediately discontinued her hormones.

After Chicago, my housemate and I landed jobs in Milwaukee. By watching the want ads carefully, we were first in line for a great apartment overlooking Lake Michigan. The only shortcoming was that we couldn't take possession for a month.

Finding temporary living quarters, especially when you have a cat, isn't easy. The boarding house we found probably didn't take pets, but we didn't ask. We took Caloma in the back way.

A month later, it was my duty to settle our account and sign out before transporting Caloma to her new home. The lobby was filled with residents sitting in a ring of chairs, a stern-looking group of elderly women and men who kept an eagle eye on what was going on in the lobby.

I settled the account with nothing being said about the cat in my arms. As I turned to leave, something made a loud, startling noise. Caloma took off like a shot with me in pursuit. As she was about to escape, I made a flying leap and slid across the floor on my belly. I grabbed Caloma, stood up and departed with as much dignity as I could muster.

If our audience had any reactions, I never knew. I can't imagine there weren't a few smiles behind their fans.

Despite her illnesses, Caloma lived a reasonably long cat life. She was always a delight—and a good friend. When we went our separate ways, my housemate let me take Caloma, recognizing that I was a cat lover while she had a preference for dogs.

Ella Ingle

Greta Bryan

My small, rural Iowa birthplace, unnoticed by the neighboring capital city of Des Moines, eschewed the average when it came to memorable characters per capita.

Ella Ingle was known the entire length and width of our town. We're talking eight blocks east to west and six blocks north to south before heading out into the countryside, alive with farms and cornfields. El lived with her spinster sister Anna and bachelor brother Bill, across Main Street from Charley Graves's store, just two doors down from my house.

To stop here would leave you with no picture of El; however, even a simple description cannot capture this poor and demented soul. She was rail thin, always wore black, including a black gauzy turban, which often leaked wisps of white hair. Hanging limply on a childlike, bent frame was always a shapeless, gunnysack dress with sleeves reaching down and swiping her gnarled, surely arthritic knuckles. Black cotton stockings wrapped her legs into substantial oxfords of the same color to complete her outfit.

Black, beady eyes were the dominant feature on her small, almond-colored, gaunt face, eyes that missed nothing as she watched from her street window, day in and day out. She rapped on her window, used hand signals and guttural sounds to communicate, smelled bad—and get this—she appeared to have no teeth, but chewed, perhaps gummed, cotton balls dipped in something antiseptic.

But all that aside, ask any Altoona kid to describe El. Two words: a witch. Halloween was especially active on her corner. While the older, undisciplined kids were dumping toilets and soaping windows, she spent the night darting furtively from her house to her cave and beyond to her outhouse, chasing off taunting kids with a broom and screaming unintelligible threats. She scared the be-jeezus out of every kid in town; in fact, the faint of heart refused to walk by the only dark-brown, two-story, ramshackle house in the town.

Everyone—except my brother Don and me.

From an early age, our mother, the community's self-appointed "meals-on-wheels," demonstrated her Christian charity by, you guessed it, providing El food, delivered by two not-always-charitable kids. But we had another connection: El housed cats—lots of cats. Male cats. Whenever a cat wandered into our yard from out in the country, Don and I lifted its tail to check El's requirements and if its plumbing was in place, we hauled it, nervously to her door. When she concurred, through inspection, that our diagnosis was correct, she pulled out a dirty rag from her sleeve, unwound it and produced her standard payment of fifty cents.

So, what makes us remember someone so insignificant on the world scene, someone who did nothing to merit print in any newspaper or book, someone who had no speech, someone who looked bad, smelled bad, lived in bad conditions? What makes us remember such folks and often forget those who have accomplished so much? Just maybe it's the small day-to-day stuff of our growing up in a small town—unnoticed.

GLIMPSES OVER OUR SHOULDERS —AND INTO THE FUTURE

Straight from Hollywood

During World War II, I was a woman Marine stationed at Camp Pendleton, near Oceanside, CA. Bob Crosby was also stationed there, and in 1944 his outfit was about to ship out to the Pacific.

Bing Crosby, Bob's brother, brought Judy Garland, Phil Silvers, Barry Fitzgerald, the Charioteers, and others down from Hollywood to entertain Bob and his outfit before they left. They also entertained all the Marines who could find a spot to sit on the ground around them.

When Bing sang, "Chills run up and down my spine," from the popular Jerome Kern ballad of the time "Long Ago (and Far Away)," an involuntary sigh escaped me. It got a laugh from the crowd. I don't know whether it was the song or the cool evening air. Anyway, it was a night to remember.

—Vivian Wood

A Little Love Story

As the frumpy woman walked at the senior center, methodically doing her laps, an admirer (her husband?) worked out on the stationary bicycle resting at one corner of the track. He kept his eyes on the woman each time she rounded his corner. Seemingly involved in her own thoughts, in a world of her own, the woman didn't notice his obvious attention.

As she slowed her pace rounding his corner, the admirer, after a long time of watching, burst out loudly, "Hey, good lookin'." He must have been planning this outburst. It was timed toward the end of her laps.

When the woman heard, "Hey, good lookin'," a surprised and happy smile broke out on her face, and she chuckled as she walked her last lap. This time, as she rounded the admirer's corner, she favored him with a glowing smile.

The couple left the track together. She was still chuckling while he wore a pleased and smug "cat that got the canary" smile. He held her hand as they walked to their car.

—Elaine Sievers

Wigged Out

Ah . . . the Sixties . . . Vietnam, Dallas, hippies, miniskirts, 33-cent gasoline, orange shag rugs, tall hair, and wigs . . . or, in my case, a wiglet.

Every spring in Iowa City, fifth and sixth graders in the fourteen elementary schools geared up for the annual spring track meet held at the high school. A big deal. Boys and girls alike trained and started eating right in preparation for the big day, a day to bring honor to *their* schools.

When the day arrived, my fifth graders and I were bussed across town to their "field of dreams." Collectively, they clamored to assigned bleacher seats to wait until their events were called. I remember feeling the heat of those young bodies surrounding me, sweaty hands, shallow, open-mouthed breathing, jiggling legs, clapping, and stomping as teammates completed their events.

The mile run was called. Steve Ryan, seated on the top row behind me, jumped up and, in an inexplicable maneuver, the zipper on the fly of his jeans clipped my wiglet—and off it sailed, bobby pins dangling, first up, then down through the bleachers to rest in the early growth of spring grass. Steve-the-dedicated-athlete did not wait for the outcome. The top two rows of kids, however, laughing hysterically, bumped and jumped down and between the bleachers like monkeys, vying to grab the pelt and return it to their teacher.

Sarah, the victor, snatched it, held it high, as she exited the underside of the bleachers. She climbed to where I was bent over, hiding my bed-head hair and, with royal dignity, plopped it on my head. With a minimum of fussing and re-establishing bobby pins, we once again brought respectability to a fifth-grade teacher.

And now, forty-seven years later, I wonder how many of those fifth graders remember that day when Mrs. Bryan flipped her wig. And by the way, Steve won his race, despite his temporary delay.

—Greta Bryan

V-J Day Parade

As a Woman Marine, I was stationed at Camp Pendleton during World War II. Shortly after V-J Day, our Marine Women's Battalion took part in a victory parade held in central Los Angeles. Hundreds of uniformed service personnel from all the military camps in Southern California participated at the giant celebration.

People lined the streets and hung from windows, cheering and throwing confetti. We were "bust your buttons" proud to be in uniform. Despite sore feet and the hot sun, marching was a pleasure.

In that moment, I felt I was *a part of history.*

—*Vivian Wood*

Out for a Spin

A beautiful sunny day with a tad of a breeze.

A snappy red convertible with the top down, gliding along the freeway.

An elderly white-haired gentleman at the wheel, wearing a smart French beret on his head, a pleased-as-punch smile on his face.

In the front passenger seat, beside the dapper gentleman, a large and elegant greyhound-like dog sitting upright with his haunches and paws on the seat, looking like a person. Head held high to catch the breeze. Owning the seat of honor beside the driver and proudly enjoying the position.

In the rear seat behind the dog, the petite lady of the house. A quiet, genteel air about her. On her head, a fashionable straw hat tied under her chin with a soft blue scarf and, on her face, contentment and joy.

A charming sight to catch the eye, this exquisite, happy trio in the snappy red convertible, gliding along the freeway on a beautiful sunny day with a tad of a breeze.

Out for a spin.

Out for a spin, thank you.

Out for a spin, thank you . . . and life is exceptionally fine.

—*Elaine Sievers*

Sputnik

The Soviet Union launched Sputnik on October 4, 1957, and Americans worried about being left behind in the race for space.

A friend and I were vacationing in Yosemite National Park some months later. We went up to Tuolumne Meadows Campground above the Park, accessible by an unpaved winding road, one-way in many spots. We saw only a handful of people, but there were dozens of deer grazing along the edge of the meadow. When frightened, they would disappear into the woods. They seemed unperturbed when we laid out our sleeping bags.

After a bite to eat and a quick wash in a nearby stream, we crawled into our sleeping bags and watched the stars come out. We knew where to look for Sputnik and, sure enough, it appeared and crossed the sky among the splendor of zillions of stars that seemed so close to us on the mountain.

We felt privileged to catch a glimpse of history from an idyllic vantage point.

—Vivian Wood

Babies Should Come with Instructions!

Like a driver's license, a baby needs to come with a required course of instructions before parents can begin to raise the little newcomer. All parents should be required to take lessons on raising a child, caring for and feeding the child at various ages, disciplining the child, educating the child, inspiring the child.

For example, one of the first problems that arises is what and how to feed the child for a successful life, robust health, and happiness. Parents then would not be responsible for the vast numbers of obese children who find it difficult to be accepted by others—or for the child's lifelong poor health, doctors' bills, and early death.

Another problem is disciplining the child. Without discipline, the child may do whatever comes to mind. The child may run with other undisciplined children, taking whatever they do not have, thus landing in jail or prison and ruining chances for a productive career.

Failure on the part of the parents to inspire the child to seek an education for a career and future life may rob the child of his or her chances to win—a Pulitzer Prize! Become a world-renowned scientist or mathematician. Or a respected teacher, nurse, doctor, business tycoon . . . endless opportunities for a happy and productive life.

—*Cathy Deitsch*

If I Could Be Any Place Else for a Week

I sit in front of the fireplace at St. Mary's Lodge in Glacier National Park. It has snowed all night and the world is deep, silent, white. The sun has just come out and revealed all the "diamonds" in the snow and on the lake.

A book lies at my fingertips—a good book—but I prefer to sit luxuriating in the warmth of the fire . . . smelling the smoke.

I stuck my head out the door earlier and got a whiff of the bracing cold. I'm content now to sit and watch the blazing logs and remember visits here in my younger days.

—*Vivian Wood*

2011

Stone Age, Iron Age, Industrial Age ... now Information Age. Facebook, Twitter, Internet, reality TV, political rhetoric, and constant news updates. Every question can be answered immediately by consulting Google. Every person can be reached on his or her cell phone. Every place can be found with a GPS. Where do we go from here?

—Judy Neigoff

About The Authors

Mary Graham Bond

Mary served as a high school librarian for twenty years at Long Island, New York. She previously worked as an editorial assistant at the Public Affairs Committee of the Alfred P. Sloan Foundation in New York City. Her published credits include articles in the *The New York Times* and *Newsday*; articles and poetry in juvenile magazines; feature writer for *Thousand Lanes Magazine*.

Bonnie Boyce-Wilson

Social worker, writer, hiker, public speaker, world traveler, university professor, private pilot, political activist, Bonnie enjoys writing about her travel experiences. She has served as a judge in writing competitions and is a past editor of the Northwest Valley Branch *Currents* newsletter. She loves music, is an outdoor enthusiast, and creates ceramics.

Greta Bryan

Greta and her husband, Dr. Hal Bryan, ophthalmologist, volunteered two-to-four weeks each year for fifteen years providing critical surgical eye care to grateful patients, primarily in Africa (Sierra Leone, Ghana, Kenya), but also in Haiti, the Philippines, and on the Mercy Ship in Central America. Hal and Greta, a retired elementary teacher, and more recently retired YMCA youth project director, divide their time between Yakima, Washington, and Sun City West, Arizona.

Cathy Deitsch

A graduate of Maryland University, Cathy later taught Home Economics and English as well as other courses on the West Coast. Following retirement, she organized and participated in a highly successful AAUW Branch Project for ten years to mentor four groups of Dysart District girls, from middle school through college, helping them realize and develop their potentials through education.

Joan Fedor

After earning advanced degrees in British and American Literature from the University of Washington in Seattle, Joan taught literature and writing at Highline College in Demoines, WA. Creative Writing classes at UW, including one from the contemporary poet and novelist David Wagoner, which increased her interest in writing. She enjoys reading and considering contemporary writers in comparison to the canon of literary history.

Anne Levig

Anne is writing her memoirs. She has published a family history and developed a text for Swedish language learners. As a free-lance writer, she focuses on a wide variety of personal travel experiences.

Greta Manville

Greta is the author of mystery and suspense novels. As a Steinbeck Fellowship project undertaken in 2002, she has written and still updates the John Steinbeck online secondary bibliography published by San Jose State University. She also acts as bibliographer and reviewer for the journal *Steinbeck Review*.

Virginia McElroy (d. 2002)

Virginia graduated *cum laude* from the University of Minnesota with a Master's degree in Theater. After she retired to Arizona, she became active in local theater. She portrayed Arizona historical figure Sharlot Hall in many performances around the state. Virginia served as President of AAUW branches in both Minnesota and Arizona. Despite personal tragedies—the loss of her husband, a pilot shot down during World War II, her twenty-two year old son, and a few years later one of her identical twin daughters—Virginia's spirit remained undaunted.

Ethel McNaughton
Born in Dundee Scotland, Ethel emigrated with her husband Archie to Ottawa, Canada, then to the United States. An advocate of Life Long Learning, Ethel attended Wayne State University in Detroit while working full time, graduating *cum laude* in Library Science and with an M.S. Degree in Archival Administration. Ethel and Archie founded a new branch of the Royal Scottish Country Dance Society in Michigan before retiring to Arizona.

Judy Neigoff
Judy moved to Arizona ten years ago from Chicago. Before she retired and unable to have children of her own, Judy spent her adult life working as a physical therapist with handicapped children in the school system. Besides work, Judy makes stained glass windows, travels, works for charities, and occasionally writes.

Evelyn Shipley
Evelyn's diverse career as a professional singer (soprano), bookshop manager, surgical assistant to oral surgeons, and corporate interviewer/recruiter took her from Ohio by way of New Jersey, Texas, and New Mexico before she retired to Arizona.

Elaine Sievers
Elaine's material evolves from a career in education and from many interests and hobbies. She and her husband maintain three acres of gardens, grass, and trees in Minnesota during the summer months. Gardening is interspersed with many hours of reading, travel, music, and theater interests. Arizona living is an important and happy part of her life. Elaine has published professionally and looks forward to more creative writing endeavors.

Ann Winsor
Following graduation from Bridgewater Teachers College in Massachusetts, Ann pursued a career as a teacher. As an envoy with SERVAS promoting world peace, she traveled to Denmark, Norway, Sweden, and Poland. She is a local representative for the Unitarian Univeralist United Nations Organization.

Vivian Wood

Vivian wrote many journal articles and book chapters in her "publish or perish" life at the University of Wisconsin-Madison. Now, retired in Sun City, Arizona, she is trying her hand at lighter stuff. She is one of the writers for the monthly column, "Women's Watch," in the Daily News-Sun. She also is working on her memoirs.